Interrupted

The Joy and Mystery of a God-Directed Life

A Memoir

By Kathrine Lee

To the reader:

I am honored you chose to read my story. It is important to me to let you know, it was written for my children as if I am journaling to them. I am aware there are grammatical errors, changes in verb tense and many other faults. As we began to edit, something I consider tragic occurred. I lost my voice. In the age of perfectionism and polishing everything, I saw I would lose my authentic voice if I attempted to craft this as a writer rather than "speak" it as a mother. I hope you enjoy it, as it was written from the heart.

Kathrine Lee

Kathrine Lee is a gifted communicator, dear woman of God and beautiful friend. She has an amazing ability to cheer people on to become who God designed them to be by communicating life changing stories wrapped in God's truth. Kathrine Lee is changing the world one life at a time.

Lysa TerKeurst – President of Proverbs 31 Ministries and New York Times Best-Selling Author

To my beautiful children, Corryn, Logan and Hannah,

When my friend, Lysa TerKeurst, wrote the quote on the previous page and front of this book, my first thought was, "First and foremost, may that be true of me on behalf of my kids." I pray these stories will cheer you on to become who God designed you to be. May *His Truth* change your life. This is your legacy.

For years people have asked me to write a book. I have always sensed God holding me back. That is, until now. I know that I am to write this book, to the three of you – the greatest gifts God has ever given me. If anyone else reads it, that is an honor.

This is for you. To share with you the story of my life. My friend, Cheri Stabile, said to me once, "I love to watch the way you let God interrupt your life. It seems like you just listen and move when and where He tells you, regardless of whether it seems to disrupt your plans." I've thought a lot about that. I even looked up the definition of interrupt. This is what I found:

Interrupt: to cause or make a break in the continuity of; to break off or cause to cease; to stop in the midst of doing something; to interfere with action or speech.

In the past I looked at being interrupted as a bad thing, as most people do. But years ago, I remember reading these words in the book of Isaiah, "Whether you turn to the right or to the left, you will hear a

voice behind you, saying, 'This is the way, walk in it'."
When I first read that, I prayed, "May that be true of
me. I want to hear Your voice. I want to go where You
want me to go, see what You want me to see, say what
You want me to say and hear what You want me to
hear."

I had lived much of my life until that time striving. I
lived in a stage of busyness, fear, confusion and
mediocrity. Those were the things that directed me
rather than the voice of God. This book is meant to
share with you where my own choices took me versus
where a God-directed life led me. To share the lessons
derived from the years I tried to control my own life
and what occurred after I gave it over to the One that
created it. You will see stark contrasts in the
difference.

A new reality of the word 'interrupt' began to form in
my mind. Since praying that Isaiah 30:21 prayer, I
came across another definition, normally related to a
computer term, that seemed to relate to the pattern I
was seeing in my life as God directed me:

Interrupt: A signal that breaks the flow of program
execution and transfers control to a predetermined
location so that another procedure can be followed or
new operation carried out.

I want to live in a way that God is the one controlling
the predetermined path that I can follow. I want to

carry out the plan He has for my life. The more I walk with God the more I understand the truth, "His ways are higher than my ways and His thoughts higher than my thoughts" (Isaiah 55:9). Proverbs 16:9 says, "A man's heart plans his way, but the Lord directs his steps." We all have plans and thoughts, and because we are made in God's image, we can do great things. Yet, I have found that if I plan, then pause and pray before I step forward, giving God precedence to interrupt those plans, it always works out better than I could have ever imagined. Pray, plan, pause, pray again and get perspective, that is the best way to move in life. If I allow Him to break the flow of my plans and transfer the control to Him, a greater procedure or operation can be carried out.

We are all wired with amazing capability, but when we allow God to animate that wiring through His inspiration and Spirit, miraculous things happen. (This proves Ephesians 3:20 to be true: "**HE** is able to do immeasurably more than all we ask or imagine, according to **HIS power** that is at work within us." Emphasis mine)

I have made many mistakes that have interrupted my life. Other people have made mistakes that hurt me and interrupted my life. Those are the kinds of interruptions that are painful yet I have learned that, by the grace of God, He can still use those for purpose, depending on how we respond. But the best parts of my story are when I allow myself to be interrupted and directed by the ways of God (found in the Bible) and the voice of God (learned in the Bible and in prayer). To follow are the stories of both: stories interrupted by pain and others from pure intentions but all have been used for purpose.

This is not just my story. It is OUR story. I have taken time out and interrupted the normal flow of life to share these with you. My life means very little if I don't pass this on to you. It means everything if I can transfer the truths hidden within these events to you. The greatest treasures I could ever impart to you are contained in the following pages.

I love you more than words can say.

-Mom

My prayer for you:

(Ephesians 3: 14-20; Colossians 1:9-12)

When I think of all this, I fall to my knees and pray to the Father, the Creator of everything in heaven and on earth. I pray that from His glorious, unlimited resources He will empower you with inner strength through his Spirit. Then Christ will make His home in your hearts as you trust in Him. Your roots will grow down into God's love and keep you strong. And may you have the power to understand, as all God's people should, how wide, how long, how high and how deep His love is. May you experience the love of Christ, though it is too great to understand fully. Then you will be made complete with all the fullness of life and power that comes from God. Now all glory to God, who is able, through His mighty power at work in us, to accomplish infinitely more than we might ask or think.

So I have not stopped praying for you... I ask God to give you complete knowledge of His will and to give you spiritual wisdom and understanding. Then the way you live will always honor and please the Lord, and your lives will produce every good fruit. All the while, you will grow as you learn to know God better and better.

We also pray that you would be strengthened with all His glorious power so you will have all the endurance and patience you need. May you be filled with joy, always thanking the Father. He has enabled you to share in the inheritance that belongs to his people, who live in the light.

(Note: I'm going to share with you story after story of God's leading and the lessons He taught me along the way. It may not be in exact chronological order because some stories weave into others more seamlessly and make the most sense if I tell them together and how they're connected. I am sharing these stories with you to show the faithfulness of God, the grace of His ways and the truth of His Word.)

Table of Contents

Lost, then Interrupted

When I was a little girl my mom took me to a swap meet. Back then swap meets were not the cool, "in" thing to do. Though they were a little sketchy, my mom and her friend were there to find a treasure hidden in the junk. As we strolled through, I remember being drawn to this piece of furniture that had a lot of little drawers (Corryn, you would have loved it). I walked over to open each drawer, hoping to find my own treasure. And I did, a button. I was so excited I turned around to show my mom, but she was gone. I was lost and began to panic. At that moment, I was interrupted by an African-American police officer who walked up and asked, "Are you lost?"

I told him yes and he proceeded to tell me that we should just sit on a nearby bench. He explained to me that if I kept walking around looking for my parents and they were walking around looking for me, that we could easily miss each other. But if, instead, we sat quietly in one place they would eventually find me.

I remember a great sense of peace as I looked into his kind eyes and held his hand. Then he pointed behind me and said, "There are your parents."

I quickly turned and saw them not too far away. I glanced back at him and smiled, let go of his hand and ran to my mom and dad. They hugged me like only parents can after losing a child and said, "That was so smart of you to stay in one place so we could find you."

I replied, "Well, he told me to." I turned to point at the officer, but he was gone. My parents said, "Who are you talking about?"

I proceeded to tell them about the police officer who told me to sit on the bench. They responded by saying that no one had been sitting there with me when they saw me. Now remember, I was holding his hand and I looked into his eyes just before I ran to them only a few yards away. To them it made no sense, but it did to me. I boldly and clearly stated, "Oh, that must have been my guardian angel." Only the faith of a child could be that assured.

Of course, my parents thought there must be a reasonable explanation so they went to the office of the swap meet and asked about any security officers that might be on duty. They were quickly informed that there were no security or police officers on site. And I responded again, "It was my guardian angel."

They didn't get it and I didn't get why they couldn't get it. So we just didn't talk about it again.

But that didn't stop me from blowing kisses every night to my guardian angel and his "family." And I always saved one BIG kiss for last. When my parents asked me who that one was for, I would respond with a big smile on my face, "Jesus." I think they thought I was a little crazy, but we did start attending church soon after. After some time, my mom came home one day and I said to her with delight, "Oh Mom! You have Jesus in your heart!" to which she responded, "How did you know?" (She had given her life to Christ that day.)

I simply answered her, "I see Him in your eyes." Jesus had interrupted my mom that day and sent her on a new pathway. I was so happy.

Interrupted by Identity Theft

There were many other times that I felt and sensed a deep connection to God and I happily went to church for a few years. But then some tragic things happened. Our pastor had an affair and my parents started having big marital problems. It seems like everyone I knew that was a "Christian" was falling. And when they fell, so did my faith. I look back now and see that the problem was that I was looking at them instead of Christ. I don't know quite when that happened but I do know that, although I knew Bible stories and verses, I was never actually taught how to study the Bible. I was never taught how to find the love and character of God there. Instead, I was taught to learn from the pastor and look at other Christians as the standard of God.

There's an inherent problem with that. They are not God. I was building my faith on them instead of the Author of my faith. I was looking to them for a standard instead of looking to the Perfecter of my personal journey.

Looking back, I can see that this is where my life got way off track. I began to look at other people for my faith instead of to the One in whom all faith should rest. I believe it is the greatest identity theft of our time: people walking around with the NAME of Christ but not displaying the character or heart of Christ. I think it is very important to have a community of people that enhance and challenge our faith journey, but they cannot be the foundation of our faith. This belongs to God and God alone.

Interrupted by Frauds

Because of my lost faith and the pain of my parents splitting up, I drifted very far away from God. I did so many things I am not proud of. I stole things, I lied, cheated and gossiped. I tried to find fulfillment in relationships with guys. I tried anything that would comfort me for the moment, but they all turned out to be frauds.

Then I met Michael when I was 16 and thought that love would save me. I'll never forget the day I met him. My friend, Nancy, was dating a guy from our neighboring small town. She wanted to go to the lake so she could hang out with her boyfriend but she needed a friend to go with her to hang out with the other guy who was there with him. I told her in no uncertain terms, "I am not going to some lake house to meet a hick from Willis."

Well, Nancy is very persistent and I finally said, "Fine! I'll go but you'd better have some alcohol there to get me through this evening." We pulled up to the lake house about an hour later and Nancy quickly jumped out of the car to go hang out with her boyfriend. So I was left sitting there in my VW Bug when I saw some guy walking up to the car from the lake.

He was wearing Wrangler jeans that were tucked into his cowboy boots. He wasn't wearing a shirt and had the biggest belt buckle and cowboy hat I had ever seen. He sauntered up to the car, spit some tobacco and said, "I understand you didn't want to meet some hick from Willis."

That was it. I was in love. Not because of the way he was dressed but because he called me on my stuff. (By the way, I never saw him dressed like that again. He had gone all around his neighborhood rounding up that get-up as a joke.)

We went out on a boat and he put on Jimmy Buffet's song, Margaritaville, pulled out a pitcher of margaritas and said, "I also understand that you need some alcohol to get through this evening."

I don't think I drank a drop that night but I certainly took in every moment I could with him. By the end of the evening, we both knew we were crazy about each other. We raced through many more days, weeks and months, spending as much time as we could together. Michael was like no guy I had ever met before. He had this way of living that was exciting and he had a way of getting me to step out of my comfort zone and do things I never thought I'd do. He taught me to ski, to dance, to cook and a lot about romance.

But there was a lot I didn't know about Michael. He had his authentic side but he also was a fraud in a lot of ways. He was a guy in a lot of pain from his childhood. He, too, was trying to fill voids in his life with things that didn't last. We had a lot of fun together but he was doing things and hiding them from me because he "didn't want me to get hurt." But the truth has a way of being revealed and I eventually found out that he was dealing and doing drugs. He was arrested and my world fell apart.

There were months of rehab and court dates and lots of pain. Eventually, I couldn't handle it anymore and I called my mom in California (they had moved there after I graduated from high school) and told her to come get me. I spent three days driving from Texas to California crying. I still loved him but just knew I couldn't go on like this.

In California, I still missed him but was trying to build a new life at the same time. I continued to go to all the things that I thought eventually would fill me up (guys, drinking, career) but everything always came up short. I kept in contact with Michael and even went back to see him once. After a day of being there, I could see things still had not changed for him so I cut my trip short and went home heartbroken again... and pregnant.

It was the shock of my life. I had no idea how to handle it. Michael was back in Texas facing more court dates and still struggling with his demons and now I was back in California, 19 years old and pregnant with his child. I had no choice but to tell my parents (who had gotten back together after a brief separation.) Their responses could not have been more opposite. My mom was upset but always valued life. So she began to plan a wedding with Michael. My father, on the other hand, was having conversations with me about how difficult my life was going to be with a guy like Michael and now a child. He told me he would either cut me off financially or he would take me to get an abortion. After weeks of agonizing, I told my dad to take me.

I will never forget walking up to the abortion clinic. There were people claiming the name of Christ but screaming things at women going in that were nothing like Christ. They were participating in the identity theft. My father placed his arm around me, I put my head down and we walked up the sidewalk. They didn't scream anything at me. I think my dad was giving them the "I dare you" look. He was a big guy and very intimidating. Ironically, I had never felt more protected by my dad yet he was walking me toward death.

After the procedure, my dad took me home and I spent the next two days on the floor of my room in the fetal position, not because of the physical pain (although there was a lot of that) but more because of the indescribable void and shame I felt. I eventually called Michael and said, "There's no wedding and there's no baby. I never want to talk to you again." And for fifteen years, I didn't.

Interrupted by Marriage and Babies

Weeks after the abortion I tried to go on with my life as if nothing had happened. I shut Michael and the memory of that day into a deep dark place in my mind. I threw myself into work and anything I could find to numb the pain. I hated being alone so I went to every social activity possible. Anything to avoid facing the silence and myself.

One evening, Phil, a friend of mine, invited me to the local softball field to watch the guys from our workplace play. Afterward, he invited a few people to his house. One of the guys caught my eye. His name was Paul. I remember we stopped at the store to buy beer and I asked him what brand he liked and he responded, "I don't drink; I'm Mormon." I didn't quite know how to respond to that so I just said, "Oh."

When we got to Phil's house. your (Corryn & Logan) dad opened a beer and I started to understand his personality. He was always making jokes and having fun. By the end of the evening, he asked me out and I said yes. We dated for a while and then moved in together after only a few months. Eventually we were married.

Corryn and Logan, here are a few things you may not know. I loved your dad. The problem is I loved him from a broken place and I think he did the same. Our relationship was based on hanging out with friends and there was not really much depth between us.

Corryn, when you were born, I learned the power of a wonderful and sacred interruption. And I saw a side of your dad I had never seen. He cried and was so tender with you. He was very loving and extremely protective. He's always been so proud of you and adored you from day one.

During my pregnancy with you, Logan, your dad was on cloud nine. He was so excited to find out he was having a boy. He couldn't wait to meet his "man cub." I'm surprised he didn't name you Mowgli. Naming you Logan was his idea. I absolutely love your name. It wasn't until later that I learned he named you after Wolverine. So like your dad. Again, I saw a tenderness and joy when you were born, Logan.

We stayed together because of the blessing of you two. He was, and still is, so proud of his son and daughter. Yet, our marriage was struggling.

Interrupted by an Untimely Death and New Name

Then came a day that changed our lives forever. Our friend, Susan, knocked on our door very early on a morning in June 1994. I opened the door to see her sobbing and she choked out the words, "Kelly and the baby died last night." I couldn't believe my ears and stood there in shock. Our precious friend, who was nine months pregnant had had an aortic aneurysm. You cannot imagine the devastation that we walked through those next few days. None of us knew how to cope.

We went to the funeral a few days later and saw precious baby Sydney lying next to her beautiful mama. There are no words. I have never seen so many grown men cry and fall to their knees. Your dad, Phil, Randy and Cameron were all pallbearers and I really don't know how they did it. We all cried together but really didn't know how to process all the feelings we were having. We went over to Pastor Chuck and Frida's house and he told us that Kelly had secretly been meeting with him, had given her life to God and had even been baptized. I've always wondered why she never felt she could share that with us but I assume it's because none of us had any interest in "religious" things at the time. But somehow, God had called her in preparation to go Home.

I remember coming home from her funeral and getting down on my knees. I mean, I literally knelt down and prayed to God. Honestly, I challenged God. This was my prayer, "WHAT AM I SUPPOSED TO DO WITH THIS?!?! Are You even real? Are You the good and loving God I believed in as a child? If so, please prove it to me. And if You are real, I want you to take over my life. I'm not doing a very good job here. Please help me."

Something interesting happened in that moment. I remembered a verse I hadn't heard for over a decade, "Seek and you will find."

And so I continued to pray, "If that's You, God. I will seek You but please make it obvious." I love to say "He's been a show-off ever since." But I want to explain why I say that. I made the commitment that day to turn my life back over to God. But I also made the commitment to live expectantly and asked Him to open my eyes to see Him. And I did. I saw Him in a sunrise and in a sunset. I saw Him in the waves of the ocean. I saw Him in your beautiful face, Corryn. (And in yours too, Logan, when you were born just a few short months later.)

I "heard" something else on my knees that day. It was the words, "Pure Hope." It was like God gave me a new name in that moment. A very personal name because that is what my mom named me. Yet up until that moment, it was certainly not how I felt. See, my first name, Kathrine, means "pure." And my middle name, Nadine, means "hope." So when I felt those words whispered in my heart I knew two things. One was that I knew God saw me. The other was that there was a calling on my life related to that name, though I had no clue what it was. In May of 1996, I received a glimpse of it that I drew in my journal. It was a place where people would come to feel love, discover their purpose, feel a sense of family and be equipped to make an impact. God wouldn't reveal the bigger purpose for another eighteen years.

Interrupted with Provision

Following that day on my knees were many exciting days, along with some very painful ones. I continued to live expectantly and God continued to show up and show off. I bought a Bible and started studying the stories that had been fed to me as a kid. I began to read the practical wisdom in Proverbs and the life-changing words of Jesus in the New Testament. I looked for a church. Your dad was adamant that he would have the final say of what church we attended. He didn't want to go with us, but wanted to make sure he felt good about where I was taking you.

I finally found one that I thought your dad would like. I invited him to come to give his stamp of approval as our home church. He came and when the service was over, I looked to get his feedback. He responded, "This isn't the church for you and the kids."

I said, "Ok. Mind if I ask why?"

He simply said, "The pastor never read from the Bible, not one time. I think if you go to church, the pastor should read from the Bible."

 To this day, I don't know where that came from, as you know your dad is not a "church guy." But somehow, in that moment, God used him to move us to the right place. I believe God honored your dad's love for you by giving him supernatural insight that you should be raised on the Truth of the Word of God, not on the opinions and rhetoric of a man calling himself a pastor. I will forever be grateful that your dad cared enough to direct us to a different church.

God also began to bring people into my life that showed me what a relationship with God looked like. One example was a woman named Elizabeth I met at a business meeting. I walked into our meeting room and she was already there reading a book. To make conversation, I asked her what book she was reading. She slid the book across the table and said, "Take it. It's great."

I responded, "I can't take your book."

She replied, "I insist." So I thanked her, tucked it away and we had our meeting. When I got home, I took the book out and it was *Six Hours One Friday* by Max Lucado. It was about the six hours that Christ hung on the cross and modern day stories about how a life can change dramatically because of those six hours. It was the first "Christian" book I had ever read. I sat outside your bedrooms, read and prayed. It was one of the first tangible ways God was reinforcing that He loved me and wanted a relationship with me.

God showed off in other ways. I had been praying that He would teach me how to get healthy and also give me a job from home. I wanted and needed to contribute to our income but the thought of leaving you at daycare killed me. See, after Kelly died, it clarified for me what was most important in life, and for me: it was family. So I began to look for a way to work from home and I began to research what was required to be really healthy. I called your Aunt Kelly, because she was a nurse, and asked her what vitamins to take. She said she wasn't sure, she would look into it and call me back. I also shared with her that I was looking for a way to work from home and asked if she had any suggestions. She said she didn't know of anything but she would be praying for me.

Just a short time later she called me and said, "You're not going to believe this but I just got a Christmas letter from my friend, Wendy. She is a rep for a company that found a way to put fruits and vegetable in a capsule–much more nutrition than just an isolated vitamin. AND I think this could be a way for you to work from home." I knew everyone needed more fruits and veggies. And I was excited to find out how I could stay at home with you two but still contribute to our family's income.

I did very well with the Juice Plus company and quickly made enough money to be home with you. But God didn't stop there. As I continued to seek Him and His direction for our lives, He began to teach me a new way to live. I no longer wanted to fight and argue with your dad anymore. I wanted to honor him and was doing everything I could to make that happen.

I remember one day we began to argue and I stopped and said, "I don't want to do this. Let's take a few minutes and talk about it when we've had time to think."

I have to admit, I went into our room to pray and "tell on him" to God. My prayer began, "Lord, don't You see how he is treating me?" I felt an immediate interruption with the words spoken to my heart, "Go make him his favorite meal." I knew right then that had to be God. Why? Because I hate to cook and I certainly did not want to cook for him right then. But that is the heart and character of God: to serve. So, I went off to the store to buy the ingredients for that favorite meal.

Once at the store, I went to the produce section, grabbing the first ingredients for that meal, when a woman said to me, "Do you think there is any nutrition in this stuff by the time we get it?"

We began to talk and I found out her name was Deana. She was an aerobics instructor at my gym and I just loved her spunk. I quickly realized she was very intrigued by the concept of fruits and veggies in a capsule because of her concern about the nutritional status of her family. We talked for quite a while and then exchanged contact information.

I got home that night and made your dad's favorite meal. I don't think we argued anymore that day. And that woman in the store ended up being one of my best friends and partnering with me in business. She and her team became a major source of income in the months and years to follow, income I was going to need.

A similar situation happened a few months later when your dad did not want me to travel to the Juice Plus conference. I had committed to him that we would make financial decisions together and that he would have the final say in areas about which we may not agree. So when the conference came up, he did not feel we had the money for me to go. I was disappointed but kept my commitment to respect whatever decision he made.

One week before the conference, he called me to say that he noticed the airlines were dropping their prices and he felt I should go to the conference after all. I double-checked that he was sure and he said, "yes." Because of booking the flight so late, I ended up having several hours to fill after the conference ended.

I asked our friend Becky if she would connect me to her sister-in-law, Lois Birner, who lived in the area. I asked if Lois could pick me up for church and then take me to the airport several hours later. Because of the conversations we had that day, Lois decided to join me in the business. She later invited her friend, Dawn Rathmann, to join the team as well. Dawn has built one of the most successful groups in the Juice Plus Company. She and many of her teammates are my closest friends. Honoring your dad led me to amazing people and provision.

Interrupted by Divorce

Although I was trying to make things better in our life, I was still living out the consequences of decisions I made when I was in pain–when I lived my life under my own decisions and control. One of the things I began to realize is that your dad didn't seem happy. I tried everything I could think of to make our marriage work. For years, I thought, "If I could just do something better or different, our marriage could get better. If I could just get in good enough shape, maybe he will love me. Or maybe if I made enough money and took the financial burden off of him, then we'd be okay." Nothing was ever enough.

Then your dad told me one day that we needed to talk but he wasn't quite ready. I wrote in my journal that day, "I feel like he just lit a fuse to a bomb but I don't know how long the fuse is or how big the explosion is going to be." At that very same time, I was going through a season in my spiritual life that was very difficult.

Every time I read the Bible it made no sense to me. All of a sudden it just seemed like a foreign language. And when I prayed, I felt like the prayers were hollow and not heard. I could not feel the presence or peace of God no matter what I did. I called my friend, Julie, and told her what I was experiencing and she said, "Kathrine, God didn't say to read the Bible and pray so you would feel something. He simply said to read the Bible and pray. So keep doing that and see what happens." So, I did. But still no feelings, encouragement or revelation would come. I felt incredibly lonely.

Then the one of the saddest day of my life came when your dad said he was ready to talk. He proceeded to tell me he was leaving. That night I laid in bed absolutely devastated. There are no words to describe the deep sadness I experienced. The only thing I knew to do was to pick up my Bible and pray. So, I did it one more time. Amazingly, the words on the pages poured over me with peace and assurance. I felt the presence of God like I never had before. I felt the Lord whisper to my heart, "I had to hide My face from you for a season so that you could see that you could be with someone yet be lonely without Me. And so that you could be alone but not lonely at all because I am with you."

There were a lot of painful days over the next several months but God taught me many lessons during that time. The most important was that I was to never put you in the middle of our divorce. And I was to never speak a word against your dad. I hope you can look back and see that I honored him. I certainly was not perfect in the marriage and God showed me that I had put a lot of pressure on your dad to love me in a way that only God could. I asked his forgiveness later for being so needy and I feel peace about that.

I know those days were painful for you both and pray every day that God will completely heal the pain that our choices caused you. We both love you very much and want the very best for you.

Interrupted by the Presence of God

The months following your dad's departure were a big adjustment for all of us. Thank goodness I had the Juice Plus business because it enabled me the time, freedom and income for us to be secure and to heal. We moved from our house on Catalina into the house on Sternwave. I have great memories of our times there. Nights in bed reading books together and eating healthy meals in front of the fireplace. Corryn, I recall your Hawaiian birthday party and Logan, your "bumping" down the stairs every chance you got. It was a sweet time.

Every night I would lie in bed and pray for us. I would also pray for our future. On July 25, 2001 at 10:30 p.m., I had an encounter with God I will never forget. I was in the living room at the Sternwave house when I felt the presence of God so heavily that I felt I had to get as low to the ground as possible. There was a sense of power and righteousness that I have not felt that heavy to this day. It made me realize why we cannot be in the fullness of the presence of God because our physical bodies could not handle it. I can still remember the smell of the carpet as I lay face down for I-don't-know-how-long. But when I felt it lift, I grabbed my journal and wrote:

Our Families

Our Bodies

Our Spirits

Our Minds

Our Hearts… are subtly being murdered and WE ARE ACTING LIKE IT'S NOT HAPPENING.

God says, "THIS IS A WAR! BUILD THE ARMIES! Men need to learn to be men again.

Women need to learn to be women again.

Children need to learn to be children again.

Then – only then – will the family survive.

When the family survives – the war can be won!"

I had no idea what to do with that but knew it was part of the calling on my life. I felt completely inadequate but was willing to follow God as He showed me what this all meant.

Just minutes later, this was my email devotional that came through at 11:06 p.m.: (God's Daily Word -Steve Troxel)

"Chapters 6-8 of Judges tell of Gideon, the fifth judge of Israel. Gideon was chosen by God to lead a small army to victory. Gideon became a hero of the people and ruled Israel as a Judge for 40 years. However, the mighty hero had a less than valiant beginning.

After being oppressed by the Midianites for seven years, the people of Israel were defeated physically, emotionally and spiritually. They felt abandoned by God and were completely without hope. In fact, when the Angel of God called, Gideon was threshing wheat at the bottom of a winepress so he would not be seen by the Midianites.

Judges 6:14-15

"The Lord turned to him and said, 'Go in the strength you have and save Israel out of Midian's hand. Am I not sending you?' "But Lord,' Gideon asked, 'how can I save Israel? My clan is the weakest in Manasseh, and I am the least in my family."

Gideon was scared and saw himself as pretty worthless, but God saw the next deliverer of Israel. Gideon saw weakness, but God saw strength. Gideon saw his past failures and present fears, but God saw the future victories of a mighty warrior.

The scientific community tells us that birds see a different spectrum of light. A flower that looks dull and boring through our eyes can be alive with "colors" as viewed through the eyes of a bird. God also sees a very unique "spectrum." Yesterday, today and tomorrow are all history to God. He sees us not only as who we are, but who we will become.

Let's put aside the baggage of our past which clouds and distorts our view. Let's refuse to look through the filter of our present understanding and perceived limitations. God has called each of us into His Kingdom and given us an assignment which will be used to bring Him glory. He sees our full potential, so let's answer the call and move forward in confidence... let's trust His vision."

I had no idea that, years later, God would use the story of Gideon to confirm the specific purpose of this calling.

Interrupted by a Vision

Sometime later I was down at the beach, spending time in prayer and worship, when, all of sudden, a "vision" of me sitting on stage talking with Oprah played through my mind. The only way I know to describe it is that it was like recalling a memory though you know it hasn't happened yet. I immediately prayed, "God, if that is You, make it come true. If it is not, let me forget about it."

I never forgot about it. Every time I thought of it, it was as vivid as the first time. But I didn't feel an urgency to do anything. I was very clear that I did not want to be famous; but I did want to have influence, so I trusted God to guide me in the next steps. I simply gave the vision back to Him and asked Him to make it come to fruition or prompt me to do something if it was His will.

It was seven years after the first "vision" that I was at the same beach spending time in prayer when I felt God prompt me, "It's time to submit your story to

Oprah." I had not been thinking about it or been in prayer for it at the time. God just interrupted my thoughts. I had an incredible peace mixed with passion. I knew it was time to take action. I knew it was God.

I went home, quickly summarized my story, and popped the letter in the mail. I called my mom and let her know what I had done, then handed the outcome back to God. I honestly forgot about it until a short time later when they called me and invited me to be on the show. God made a way to fulfill the vision He gave me. It was an amazing time, not because we were on Oprah, but because we were walking in the midst of God fulfilling a promise.

The first time I was on the show, it didn't look like the vision. I was on the show but I was standing talking with Oprah and Bob Greene, not sitting and talking with just Oprah. I remember when the show was done, everyone asking me how it was. I responded, "It was incredible but I'll be on again." I did not say that from an ego-centered place. I spoke it from a Christ confidence that what He began, He would finish. I knew by now to take God at His word. And sure enough, the show kept in touch with me and years later they invited me back. This time it looked exactly like the vision. Just Oprah and I on the stage talking about how to love yourself. Once again, God was showing off.

I remember being in the hotel room the morning after the show, writing in a journal Oprah had given me. I was thanking God for bringing the vision to reality but also seeking Him again for what was next. I distinctly remember the peace that washed over me and Him speaking these words to my soul. "Enjoy your life, Kathrine, and live in the Mystery of what I AM going to do next." Wow! What peace and excitement! I would soon learn that living in the Mystery of God is the greatest adventure you can ever experience!

Interrupted to Forgive

At the same time God was revealing the future, He was also working in and through me to heal the past. During the time I was married to your dad, and after I committed my life to Christ, God began to reveal the painful things of my past so He could heal them. The biggest one being the abortion. At different moments in my quiet prayer and worship times with God, He would gently bring those memories to mind so that I could grieve over them and feel his forgiveness. He began to exchange my pain and shame for love and purpose.

I found myself praising God because of the assurance I felt that I would meet the baby someday. I remember praying, "God, please tell my baby I love it." And God spoke to my heart, "Kathrine, he is your son. It's a boy." Tears of joy still fill my eyes as I type this. The same kind that come in a delivery room when you hear the doctor say, "It's a boy."

Then my prayers changed to, "Please tell my son I love him and can't wait to hold him someday." One day I felt God say, "His name is Joshua, Kathrine." WOW! God named my son! I felt God gently say, "Someday you will need to call Michael and ask for his forgiveness. Joshua is his son, too. But now is not the time." Just like other promptings from God, I knew it was His will but had also come to know that His timing is as perfect as His will. So, I waited.

Almost a year after the divorce was final, God prompted me one morning in prayer. "It's time to call Michael and ask for his forgiveness." I have to admit; this was one thing I did not want to do. I was much more comfortable having that part of my past, especially Michael, tucked away somewhere deep in my mind. The thought of talking to him again scared me and made me incredibly sad. Yet, I had learned obeying God always brought blessing to me or someone else, usually both.

In faith, I obeyed and dialed his number. The fact that I remembered a number from fifteen years before was a miracle. The fact that Michael's voice was on the answering machine connected to that number all these years later was a second miracle.

I'm sure my voice was trembling as I left a message "following the beep." I said, "Hi Michael. This is Kathrine Newlan, used to be Kathrine Baker, a voice from your past. I am going to be in the Houston area in a couple of weeks and would like to take you and your wife out to dinner. (I had heard through the grapevine he was married.) So, if you and your wife would like to meet me, I'd love to get together. I have something I'd like to talk to you about if you and your wife can make it." See what God did there? He made sure I honored his wife. There was no way I was going to meet with him unless his wife was present.

A couple of days passed and I did not hear from him. I assumed his wife got the message and pressed "delete" as quickly as she could. And to be honest, I wouldn't blame her. For there was no way she was married to him and had not heard about our past relationship. She had every right to protect her marriage. So, I went on with great peace that I had done what God asked me to do.

On the third day, the phone rang. I answered and I heard a voice on the other end say, "You're not going to believe this!" I would recognize that voice anywhere. It was Michael. He continued, "Well, maybe you will believe it because this is how we always were. I haven't called you back because I was in California looking for you!" That's right, after fifteen years God had prompted him at the same time to find me. He had business in California and a month before he left, God had prompted him that he needed to find me. On that trip he did everything he could to find me. This was before the days of Google and Facebook and he didn't know my married name so he headed home defeated. He was on the way home, asking God, "If you wanted me to find her, why didn't you help me?" He walked in the door of his home, pressed play on the answering machine, and there was the message from me. Only God.

We began to talk about what was going on in our lives. He shared with me about his divorce and the fact that his wife had had an affair. When I asked him why she had done that I was waiting for him to list all the reasons and put all the blame on her. Instead, he simply said, "The day you called me and said there was no wedding and no baby, I shut off part of my hear. I never gave her access to my whole heart so she found someone that would." I was amazed. I couldn't believe he would take responsibility for her choice. Something about him had changed.

I proceeded to tell him I had something I wanted to talk with him about but needed to do it in person. I asked if we could meet on my next trip to Texas. He said, "What if we could meet sooner? I am going to be in California soon, actually the week of your birthday. Could we meet then?"

My heart was racing but I calmly said yes. Then I called a group of my friends and set up a dinner with all of them where he would show up. I wasn't sure I could handle being alone with him, so my friends and I set up all kinds of code words to give, whether they were to stay or go.

The day came and he walked into the restaurant overlooking the ocean in Dana Point Harbor. Within minutes I felt comfortable (but guarded) so I gave the signal that it was okay for them to leave I found myself just pouring out my heart about what God had done regarding the abortion. I went on to tell him, "Michael, God has forgiven me. And not only that, He has told me that it was a boy and his name is Joshua." Michael's eyes filled with tears and he began crying so hard that we had to leave the restaurant. We went down to the beach and talked for hours. We went through every hurt we caused each other and asked for forgiveness, and then forgave each one.

Michael also found out for the first time that my mother did everything she could to try to stop the abortion. For all those years, he thought both my mom and dad convinced me. He asked me to set up a meeting with Mom. So the next night, back to that restaurant in Dana Point Harbor we went. My mom was not exactly thrilled that Michael was back in touch with me. She really didn't want to meet with him because she knew the amount of pain he had caused me in the past. But she reluctantly showed up.

As they sat across from each other Michael broke the awkward silence. "Geri, thank you for meeting with me. I wanted the opportunity to tell you two things. First, thank you for trying to save my baby. And second, I want to ask for your forgiveness for not being the man I needed to be for your daughter so she had to make that terrible decision. Will you forgive me?" My mom was stunned. She cried and Michael cried again and I joined in. I'm sure the staff at the restaurant posted a note at the front not to let us in again.

At the end of the weekend Michael asked me, "Do you think you'll ever have with anyone else what we had together?"

I quickly answered, "Yes, the guy I'm dating right now is really special. God will give you something better than what we had together." It was great to be connected to Michael again because I had loved him so much in the past but there was no way he was getting near my heart again. Or so I thought.

Interrupted by Grace

Little did I know from the day he got the message on the answering machine, he had told his friends and family, "I'm going to marry her someday." When he got home they were all asking him how it went: "Did you tell her how you felt about her?" He answered, "She isn't ready, yet." Michael, too, had learned that God's timing is as perfect as His will.

Meanwhile, God had me studying the story of Adam and Eve. I had read it dozens of times but this time I saw something different. God highlighted to me the verse where Adam is naming the pairs of animals as they walked by him and then says to God, "But there is not one for me."

That is exactly how I felt in those days. God was parading all of these amazing couples in front of me. It was a blessing because for the first time I was seeing what healthy marriages looked like. But I, like Adam, was saying, "But there is not one for me" (the guy I was dating when Michael came back into my life had broken things off). But as he perhaps said to Adam, God said, "Someday I will wake you up and you will clearly see the one for you."

As the months went by, I wasn't dating anyone and Michael and I would connect if one of us was in the other's hometown on business but nothing about romance was ever mentioned. Not one romantic gesture or comment was ever made. We were just friends. Then one day, I was having surgery and Michael was going to be in town on business. He asked if he could come to the house and take care of me because he knew you kids would be at your dad's house and he did not want me alone following surgery. He was insistent and, finally, I reluctantly said yes.

He spent the weekend taking care of me, making me meals, cleaning up, shopping and even emptying my surgical drains (now that's attractive). He made my room into a movie theater. He asked if he could lie in bed with me to watch the movie and jokingly promised to keep one foot on the floor (which he actually did). Sunday afternoon came and it was time for him to leave. He told me goodbye and went out the door without one romantic gesture. I heard his car start and saw him drive off. That moment God gave me a revelation. It was as if God woke me up and I knew that I loved Michael. I knew he was the one for me.

But that presented a problem. I had no idea how he felt about me.

That afternoon when he landed for his layover in Phoenix, he called to check on me. I told him I was just fine, not breathing a word of what God had shown me. Then he asked me a question, "Kathrine, do you miss me?"

I started bawling and responded, "I've been crying ever since you left."

He said, "I'm going to call you when I get home. We need to talk." Those couple of hours seemed like an eternity to me. I did everything I could to pass the time. Then he called and said, "I have never stopped loving you. I will always love you. But I need to know something, could you see yourself marrying me? Because if you can't, I don't even want to begin this. I can't go through the hurt of losing you again."

 I simply responded, "I don't know for sure."

He said, "As long as it's not a no, that's good enough for me." We were married six months later.

And Corryn and Logan, you need to know he made the decision to marry all three of us. He talked to me for hours about his commitment to each of you. He worked for hours on his vows to each of you. He was the one that changed our honeymoon plans from Cabo, to the road trip with the four of us. As he put it,

"I can't marry you and immediately take you away from them for a week. They need to see my commitment is to all three of you, to be a family." He has loved you wholly and fully since day one.

A couple other fun things about our story that you may not know. When your great grandfather, Bopie, was alive, I made a vow to him that I would never marry again until a man looked at me the way he looked at Grandma Alice. I have never seen a man love a woman that beautifully. I never told anyone that I made that promise to him. Yet, about a month before the wedding, my mom said to Michael, "I'm so happy for Kathrine. You look at her the way my dad used to look at my mom." Another amazing thing is that we later realized that we got married on their anniversary.

And Hannah, I told your dad when we got married that I didn't want any more children. He agreed but was always hoping for one more. I think I never wanted to have a child just to make up for the abortion. That wouldn't be right. But after seeing how much your dad loved Corryn and Logan, God began to soften my heart. I knew that having a child with him would be to grow our family and the love between us all. And God, in His grace, gave us you.

That is why you are named, Hannah Grace. Your first name, Hannah means grace and of course, Grace means grace. So you are a double portion of God's grace to us. Not only did God let Michael and I reunite and create a family with Corryn and Logan, but he also blessed us with you. See, mercy is not getting what you deserve when you do something wrong, but grace is getting a gift on top of that. God not only forgave us but gave us you when we didn't deserve a gift.

Interrupted by Holy Yoga

Holy What? Yes, that says Holy Yoga. Let me explain.

Each year Michael likes to do something special for me on my birthday. So one year he kept asking me what I wanted to do. Did I want a girls' trip away with my friends? A weekend with him? A family party? This particular year, I could not think of anything, yet I felt there was something special coming. So I kept telling him, "I'm not sure but I know that I will know when I know."

It was now just days away from my birthday weekend and I still had nothing. I went out for my morning walk that Wednesday morning and was enjoying the silence, when I felt that still small voice whisper, "Look up Christian Yoga." Christian WHAT? "Christian Yoga." Again, I had come to know that voice pretty well so out of pure curiosity I googled, "Christian Yoga." And up popped a local group called Holy Yoga OC.

I immediately went to their statement of faith and saw it aligned with my beliefs. And then I saw it: a retreat that coming weekend, just two days away. I knew immediately that this was what I was supposed to do for my birthday. But there were a few problems. First of all, I don't "do" yoga. I'm a curvy girl and the women that practice yoga in our area are the most fit women I'd ever seen. Second of all, I get very uncomfortable walking into a party by myself, much less a whole weekend. And finally, it was two days away. There was no way they had room. I made a quick call to rule the weekend out. Surely they did not have any room and would not want to take in some random woman that didn't even own yoga pants.

A sweet voice answered the phone immediately and I stammered, "Uh- Hi, my name is Kathrine. I don't do yoga and I don't even own yoga pants but I just came across your website and was wondering if you had any room for your retreat this weekend. I'm sure you don't but I just thought I would check."

The sweet woman on the other end started laughing. I said, "What?"

She said, "I just hung up the phone from a last minute cancellation, we have one spot open."

"Uh, I guess I'm going to buy yoga pants."

I got home from my walk, told Michael what I wanted to do for my birthday. He gave me a very confused look.

"I know, I know. I don't get it either but I just know I'm supposed to go."

I called that sweet woman back (by now I've learned her name is Tasha) and explained again that I've never done even one yoga pose and I was just wondering how I was going to fit in.

She graciously replied, "We are so glad you're coming. Don't worry about a thing. We can set you up in the back if that would make you feel more comfortable. Just think of it like stretching while listening to worship music. You can do as little or as much as you want, but bring a journal. Women often hear from God while they do this so you may want to capture those thoughts."

Oh, NOW she was talking my language: stretching, worship music and journaling? That I can do. So I packed my suitcase and got on the road for the three-hour drive. I was still uncomfortable when I arrived but the women did their best to put me at ease. They explained that the weekend would be mixed with yoga, group discussion and lots of quiet time. I made the decision that I was all in for the experience.

In one of the first yoga sessions, I began to stretch and listen to the worship music. Suddenly I felt God say to me, "Lie face down and worship me for I AM your King." I'm not sure how long I was there but felt a deep impression of the Righteousness of God. Then I heard, "Move onto your knees," so I did. And then I felt as if someone was lifting my chin up and I heard, "I AM the Lifter of your head. You can look me eye to eye like a friend."

An incredible warmth washed over me. And again, I don't know how long I stayed there but I know I had a huge smile on my face that I couldn't stop if I tried. Then, again, I felt as if someone was lifting me up from underneath my arms and I heard, "Stand up and take your place in My Kingdom, My child." I knew in that very moment that God was "commissioning" me for ministry.

See, I had worked for many years in the business world but had always felt in my heart I was supposed to be in ministry. I also believed that somehow those words spoken to me when Kelly died: "Pure Hope" were supposed to be a part of it. I still didn't know what all that meant, but what I did know was God had just called me to it. I was so excited to see what He would reveal next. Little did I know that the theme of the retreat would play a major role in directing me. The theme was a word from the Bible that I had somehow never seen. Selah. I knew it was significant and held onto that word as a sacred piece of the unfolding of my calling. More about that later.

Interrupted by a Conversation
(That Turned into a Calling)

As God continued to bless our family, both Michael and I had a sense that God was calling us to a change. With the calling of ministry clearly on our lives, we began to pray and thank God for all He had done for us, ask Him to guide us in the next steps, and hold out our hands with all we owned. The posture of our hearts was: "God, you did this; what do you want us to do with it?" I was also consistently in prayer about what the meaning of Pure Hope was and how it fit into this season.

Then one day I was on a business trip and boarded my flight. As you know about me, I love my flying time to be my recharge time. Although I love people–in fact, people are my life's work–I always need to be alone to recharge. So as I boarded this flight I was excited that it seemed the seat next to me was empty. But just in case, I put on my headphones and put a faith-based book and Bible in my lap. (All of these were clear hints to the people around me that I didn't want to talk.) Sure enough, the seat next to me remained empty. That is until the very last minute when a businessman boarded and hurriedly plopped down into the seat next to me. I thought, "No problem, men never try to make small talk on a plane."

Well, I was wrong. He immediately tapped me on the shoulder. I took off my headphones just slightly, and barely turned my head toward him as if to hint, "Make it quick."

He did. He asked me some random question, I answered him with one word and put my headphones back on. He tapped me on the shoulder again and I repeated the same posture. Then a third time. And suddenly I heard that voice I had come to know so well interrupt me: "Talk to him."

I wish I could say I joyfully complied but I took a moment to argue, "Really, God? I'm tired and I don't want to talk." Silence. I knew what that meant. Obey and get a blessing or ignore and always wonder what you missed. I took off the headphones. About an hour later I realized that we were probably disturbing all the other passengers around us because we were laughing and talking so much. I thought I had it all figured out. "I get it, God. This guy is smart, handsome, charismatic, well-traveled and well spoken. He's a catch! You wanted me to talk to him so I could set him up with one of my single girlfriends. They will meet, get married, have babies and name one after me all because I was obedient to talk with him." Yes, I really did think this.

He shared with me later that he talked to me for that hour so that I would get to know him, like him and to set me up to ask one question. And I did, "What is it that you do for a living?"

I bit and he gladly answered, "I own the second largest pornography company in the world."

What? Did I hear that right? Well, setting him up with one of my friends didn't seem quite as wonderful. So, Lord, why did You have me talk with him? I immediately felt a sense of calm, peace and curiosity and simply responded, "Really? Tell me about that." (He told me later that when he saw the Bible and faith-based book on my lap, he thought it would be funny to have the "church lady" like him and then tell her what he did. He told me he thought it would be entertaining to watch me squirm or judge him the rest of the flight. But he went on to say, "Instead, you met me with love, grace and curiosity and I didn't know what to do with you.")

Now it's important to note that if you'd have told me I would be put in that position, I would have told you NO WAY. Don't do that to me. I was exposed to pornography at a very young age because my grandfather (my dad's dad) was radically addicted to it. I'll never forget the day he died. We were all surrounding his bedside and he took his last breath. I looked at my grandmother and she looked down, took a deep breath, looked up sharply and said with disdain, "Get that stuff out of my house."

After 50 years of marriage those were the first words out of her mouth. I watched my father that afternoon, while grieving the loss of his father, carrying barrels of pornography out of their house.

So, again if you would have told me that I'd be talking with this man, that God asked me to talk with this man, I would have said, "No! I can't. I won't know what to say."

But God's Word says, "Don't worry about the words you are to say, for at the appointed time they will be given to you." And they were. He told me how he got into it. Why he shouldn't be judged for it, (Funny, I wasn't judging him but he felt he had to justify his choice.) and how well he treated "his girls."

I asked him, "How do you get the girls?"

He replied quickly, "Oh, that's easy, we just send scouts out to malls and high schools and tell them to look for girls with daddy issues." I have to say that took my breath away but I continued to listen.

After listening for quite a long time, I asked for his permission to challenge him. He said, "Sure." So I made a statement and asked him a question. I said, "I believe all men are meant to be the protectors of women. I hear you have justified what you do. But I'm just wondering if ever, in the middle of the night, your hero's heart wakes up on their behalf?"

Mr. Charisma had nothing to say. He just looked at me for a minute and then looked out the window. I just sat with him in silence for quite a while. Then he turned to me and began to tell me about his wife, his daughter, his divorce…

I interrupted him with a concerned, "Oh no!"

He said, "What?"

I said, "So your daughter has daddy issues?" He looked at me wide-eyed with his head kind of rattled. In that moment I saw a realization come to him. He had never considered his own daughter could be a target. And he had never considered those girls were someone's daughter.

When we got off the plane, he said, "Kathrine Lee, I'm going to tell you two things. First of all, I don't think I'm ever going to sleep quite the same again."

I replied, "Oh good." And we both laughed.

And then he said, "And secondly, can I get your card, because I think someday my girls may need you."

It was in that moment, after almost seventeen years of wondering, I knew the purpose of Pure Hope. Not in totality but overall. It was to raise up the heroes' hearts in men. It was to teach women their value and identity. I wasn't sure what the pornography connection had to do with it but felt the sense that I needed to do some investigating. Once home, I began to research the issue of pornography in a broader way. How did it affect men? Women? The Family? Society? This is what I found:

As many as 1 out of every 4 online searches are for porn.

Every second 30,000 people are viewing pornography.

The average age of first exposure is just 11.

Pornography use increases the marital infidelity rate more than 300%.

In 56% of divorce cases, one party had an obsessive interest in porn sites.

37% of all internet traffic is pornography.

Of 8 to 16 year olds, 90% have viewed porn online (most while doing homework).

In 2006, the pornography industry revenues were larger than the total combined revenues of... "Microsoft, Google, Amazon, eBay, Yahoo, Apple, Netflix, and Earthlink." (Consider this, 90% of pornography on the internet is free, so these statistics represent only 10% of the porn industry.)

Researchers have found that users acclimate to the porn they watch - they get used to it, and it stops being exciting or arousing. Why? Because the brain's pleasure response has gotten numb. Because of the addictive nature of porn, in order to just feel some sense of normality, an individual usually needs an ever increasing dosage of porn. That is why watching porn tends to be an escalating behavior. (see FightTheNewDrug.org for more info)

It has been said that porn is the rocket-fuel that is creating the demand for trafficking.

Trafficking is the number two criminal industry in the United States and is also the fastest growing. It is predicted to surpass drug trafficking as the number 1 criminal industry in the very near future.

Overwhelmed? So was I. Seems unbelievable? I felt that way too. Asking, "How do you even begin to make a difference in something this big?" I asked that, also. The only hope and answers I received are contained in the following pages.

Interrupted by God's Broken Heart

After learning all of this information, I just cried out to God, "What do you want me to do about this?"

He answered me every morning in my prayer chair. I would sit down expecting to go through my normal rituals of prayer. I had been sitting in that same place for years and would always begin with acknowledging who God is by recounting His names and character. I would claim those things over my life. "God, You are my provider. You are my strength. You are my comforter. You are my refuge. You are my redeemer. You are the God of peace." And on it would go as I worshipped Him.

Then, I would always spend time in gratitude, thanking Him for all He has done for us. I'd recount the previous day and just sit in thankfulness. Psalm 126 was always on my mind at this time: "The Lord has done great things for us and we are filled with joy."

And then I'd spend time bringing prayer requests to Him. I always began with Michael and myself and then on to each of you kids. I'd pray for you by name and ask God to comfort or provide for you anything that you needed that day. I know that only He knows all the challenges you may be facing or the dreams you have in your heart so I consistently asked that He guide, direct and protect you. And I always ended by praying for the rest of our family and friends—for things I knew were concerning them. And finally, I closed with thanking God again for His love and guidance in my life and asking Him to reveal anything to me in His Word I needed to know.

But something was different now. As I sat down to pray, at some point God would interrupt my prayers and I'd begin to cry. I'm not just talking a few tears coming down my cheeks. These were deep, gut-wrenching tears that I couldn't stop or control. It was like God was showing me His heart over the issues I had just discovered and especially over the people trapped in it. I cried over young girls and women I had never met. I cried over men that were consumed by their draw to pornography. I cried over the women who struggle, not knowing their identity. I cried over families that were broken. And I couldn't stop it. I just sat there until God "turned it off." And then I would ask again, from a place of deep frustration, "What do you want me to do about this?"

My friend has called this my time of going into the "Weeping Room." Finally, after weeks of this, I asked God, "Is it always going to be like this? Will I always walk around with this burdened heart? I'm ok if that is what you want from me. I just need to know if I am going to carry this sadness for the rest of my life."

God quietly responded, "Kathrine, I am the God who made a platypus. You're going to have fun." Suddenly, joy bubbled up and I just started giggling right there in the same chair I had been weeping in for weeks. What I didn't realize at the time is that He was getting ready to take me into the "strategy room" and on to the greatest adventure of my life.

Interrupted by a Greater Vision

A short time later I was on a flight headed to Lubbock, Texas to work with my friend, Kathy Crockett, on a corporate account. I got on the flight as usual, buckled my seat belt, they closed the cockpit doors, and suddenly I was interrupted. What I thought would be a time of recharging, turned into "movie time." A "movie" started playing in my mind. It was just what happened regarding Oprah but this time the vision was much longer and vivid. It was a of vision of a ranch. A place of abundant beauty. There was a beautiful building that was very homey, filled with rich colors and a great sense of peace. It was a property where families could be strengthened and victims of trafficking could live and experience restoration. When we landed and they opened the cabin door, it was like the movie stopped. I quickly grabbed my journal and began writing down everything I could remember.

As soon as I got off the plane, I called Michael and said, "Remember what happened with the Oprah vision? Well, it just happened again. I have to tell you now because it is so big and overwhelming that if I don't talk about it now, I will never speak of it."

I told Michael about the "movie" with as many details as possible and he simply responded, "I'm in. Whatever it takes, I'm in."

The second I heard his strength and confidence, I felt a sense of purpose and passion like never before. I knew we were getting ready to step into the unknown but I knew that as long as we followed God's leading and stayed united, we could do anything God called us to do.

I walked out of the airport and told Kathy all about what had just happened. She immediately began to strategize and dream with me. Anyone that knows Kathy knows she is a "get it done" kind of person. She has great faith and influence and loves to connect people for a common goal, especially when that goal is going to make a positive impact on others. We went on to work with the incredible home builder, Betenbough Homes (who later gifted us with renderings of the homes that could be built on the ranch) and one thing Kathy kept saying during that visit was, "Ryan and Holly Morris are supposed to be a part of this. I just know it." I couldn't wait to meet them and see what God had in store.

When I got back to Michael I knew I was supposed to ask him one question, "What is your dream for the ranch."

He quickly responded, "It would be at least a thousand acres." Then he quickly said, "I have no idea why. That's a lot of land. But it is one thing I feel in my heart."

All I could think was, "Ok, God, this one is up to you. Please show us what to do next."

Interrupted by a Persistent Friend

Just a little while later, my friend, Genia Rogers, called me, asking me to come visit the Dream Center in Los Angeles. She had been in LA for months on business and they had been attending church services there. She said, "Kathrine, you're going to love it here. I just feel in my heart you're supposed to come visit." Well, you kids know how much I hate driving into LA, especially at night. She wanted me to attend one of the evening services so that would mean I'd be driving there during peak traffic time and driving home late at night–two things I simply do not do if I can avoid it. But Genia kept interrupting my life, requesting that I head up to LA. She even said, "I know I'm being a pain, but I just feel you're supposed to come." She was persistent and one night I finally went.

She had set up a tour of the property before we went to the church service. It is incredible what they do there. (Someday I want to take you to hear the story and experience it for yourself). At the end of the tour, they take you to a long narrow room. There are residences of the Dream Center Programs there lining each side and clapping. It is their way of thanking you for coming and caring. As I walked through the applause I felt God say, "Applause means nothing if you don't do something."

Again, I quietly asked God, "So what do you want me to do?" I heard nothing in reply.

We went on to the church service, which was amazing, and at the end of the evening, Genia said, "I want you to meet Caroline, Pastor Barnett's wife." I said, "That's nice, Genia, but I don't need to meet her. I'm sure lots of people want to connect with her after services."

But again, Genia persisted. "No, I really feel like you're supposed to meet her." We began to walk toward her and I felt God say, "Ask her specifically what to pray for."

So after introductions and a very brief conversation, I said, "Caroline, I feel like God wants me to ask you if there is anything specific I can be praying about for you."

A concerned and burdened look came over her face and she responded, "Oh, will you please pray over our Project Hope. It is our trafficking ministry and I have never seen an issue so hard on our staff. They work so hard and it's very tough. Will you pray for the staff? We really are looking for a way to encourage and equip them."

WOW! Out of all the ministries at the Dream Center (there are lots), Caroline mentions the very one God had been breaking my heart over. I quickly told her what God had been doing in my life, committed to pray and offered my help in any way possible. Genia filled her in that I was a life coach and strategist and Caroline asked if I could meet with someone the following week to see how exactly I could help. God was continuing to reveal what it was that I could do to begin to help. I later had the privilege of gifting the Project Hope staff with retreats where they can rest and be restored. We loved on them and have stayed connected and continue to support them as needed. They have also taught me so much about the issue of trafficking and several have become great friends.

Interrupted by Sacrifice

As much as I loved helping at Project Hope, I continued to see the ranch in my mind. I'd pray and ask Him to show us what step we needed to take. For quite a while it was simply to pray and wait. Then, in January of 2014, Michael and I both felt the prompting, "Put your house on the market and go to a land I will show you."

There were only two challenges about that. First, you know how much I love our home. I always thought I would be 80 years old, lying on my bed, looking out the window at the willow tree. And second, where the heck is "a land I will show you?"

I have to admit, it was a painful decision. We were willing but that didn't stop the grief. The hardest part was telling you kids because I knew how much it would hurt you but I also knew that God would take care of you. And that no matter where we lived, we are always a family. Nothing can change that. And we want all

God has for us, not what we think is best. We want His best for our lives and yours.

We set a date of February 17 to sign the papers to put the house on the market and to leave in the RV on February 18 for a road trip to look for land. We also scheduled a speaking tour along the way. At the time I had a talk entitled, "Design Your Life." It was all about how to overcome fear, failure and a frazzled brain to live a life of legacy. In the talk, I shared how staying home with you kids and working with the Juice Plus company had allowed us the option of being home raising you, which to me was the greatest legacy I could have. I also included in the talk the vision of Pure Hope Ranch as an example of another type of legacy that God was putting on our hearts now that two of the three of you had graduated high school. We were excited to set out on this new adventure and I fully expected to find the land and have our house sell while we were gone.

But before we set out, we had one event left to do in Southern California. Michael and I were hosting a Valentines Weekend Marriage retreat February 14-16. We always do a Sunday morning "church service" at our retreats but this time I didn't have a speaker. Michael kept saying he felt like I was supposed to do it. I remember telling him, "I'm speaking and facilitating all weekend. The last person they need to hear from is me." But when we couldn't find a speaker and it was Saturday night at 10:00 p.m., I finally gave in that I was the one to fill that spot.

I began to pray, "God, this is such an honor. What would you have me speak on?" At first I didn't hear anything, so I just waited (trying to stay awake). But then three worship songs came to mind and I jokingly said to Michael, "God's beginning to download. We're going to be okay." I gave him the three songs and said, "I feel like we are supposed to play these two before I speak and this one to end." The ending song was, "I Can Only Imagine."

Then I waited and felt God say, "Tell your dad's story. All of it. From his birth until now." I immediately saw the thread of the lesson God wanted me to teach. My dad's story is a story of abandonment, adoption, performance, seeking identity, failing, leaving, returning and forgiveness. It took him a long time to realize what really mattered in life and I was excited to share the tough lesson of his life but also a message of redemption. The talk just came to me in pictures and parallels that apply to all of our lives. Michael even found this great poem to summarize the theme:

What Will Matter by Michael Josephson

Ready or not, someday it will all come to an end.

There will be no more sunrises, no minutes, hours or days.

All the things you collected, whether treasured or forgotten, will pass to someone else.

Your wealth, your fame and temporal power will shrivel to irrelevance.

It will not matter what you owned or what you were owed.

Your grudges, resentments, frustrations and jealousies will finally disappear.

So, too, your hopes, ambitions, plans and to-do lists will expire.

The wins and losses that once seemed so important will fade away.

It won't matter where you came from or what side of the tracks you lived on in the end.

It won't matter whether you were brilliant or beautiful.

Even your gender and skin color will be irrelevant.

So what will matter? How will the value of your days be measured?

What will matter is not what you bought but what you built,

not what you got but what you gave.

What will matter is not your success but your significance.

What will matter is not what you learned but what you taught.

What will matter is every act of integrity, compassion, courage or sacrifice that enriched, empowered or encouraged others to emulate our example.

What will matter is not your competence but your character.

What will matter is not how many people you knew,

But how many will feel a lasting loss when you're gone.

What will matter is not your memories but the memories of those who loved you.

What will matter is how long you will be remembered, by whom and what for.

Living a life that matters doesn't happen by accident.

It's not a matter of circumstances but of choice.

Choose to live a life that matters.

I went to bed with a great peace and anticipation of being able to share it the next morning. That night, at about 2:00 a.m., my phone rang with the news that my dad had just died suddenly. My mom and brother, Brad, were headed to the facility where he lived and encouraged me to stay and finish out the weekend and just meet them later that day.

After crying the entire rest of the night, I went in the next morning and shared the story of my father's life with the beautiful couples that attended the retreat. I didn't tell them until the very end that this was not just a story of his life but also his memorial. Then I asked Michael to play the final song ("I Can Only Imagine" by Mercy Me) I was stunned when I heard the words, since, of course, the song was given to me prior to me learning of my dad's death. I had not put together the significance until it began to play:

I Can Only Imagine by Mercy Me

I can only imagine
What it will be like
When I walk
By your side
I can only imagine
What my eyes will see
When your face is before me
I can only imagine
Surrounded by Your glory, what will my heart feel
Will I dance for You Jesus or in awe of You be still
Will I stand in Your presence or to my knees will I fall
Will I sing hallelujah, will I be able to speak at all
I can only imagine
I can only imagine
When that day comes
And I find myself
Standing in the Son
I can only imagine
When all I will do
Is forever
Forever worship You
I can only imagine
Surrounded by Your glory, what will my heart feel
Will I…
Surrounded by Your glory, what will my heart feel
Will I dance for You Jesus or in awe of You be still
Will I stand in Your presence or to my knees will I fall
Will I sing hallelujah, will I be able to speak at all
I can only imagine

Only God could have orchestrated that in advance. He knows the number of our days and set out to honor my dad that day. I am still in awe.

We headed back to our home to be with the family just a few hours later. We had an important decision to make. Did we still leave for the road trip?

Our whole family decided not to have a funeral for my dad. Unfortunately, he lived a life in which he didn't have any friends but he did have us. We felt that the service I had at the retreat and our time together that afternoon was just right. We would still leave Tuesday morning to see what God had in store for us.

Interrupted by a Crisis of Faith

Tuesday morning, February 17 we loaded up in the RV to begin the road trip. I have to admit I thought I would hate it. I was doing it because it was a dream of Michael's and out of curiosity about the possible ranch properties we would see. I was also excited to share my new talk, "Design Your Life."

About three days in, I brought Michael his coffee in bed and said to him, "I think I could get used to this. It's wonderful. It's so, so..." I didn't have the words to describe it but he did.

He said, "It's simple."

And he was right. There were not the tugs of normal life, the daily routines that sometimes can wear you down. Instead it was just waking up to what would come next that particular day. Every few days we stopped in a different town or city and I would share my talk. But something interesting was happening. At the end of the talk, when I shared the vision of Pure Hope Ranch, every audience had an emotional response. People were crying, passing notes to each other or coming up to me afterwards with money or their business cards with the hope to help out.

I was stunned. I had been speaking for eighteen years at the time and had never seen an audience respond like that. The strangest part was that the segment about Pure Hope Ranch was only about 5-7 minutes of an hour-long talk. Yet, it seemed to touch people's hearts to the point of moving them to want to do something. And it freaked me out. I'm not talking about the fact that it made me uncomfortable. It literally freaked me out. It seemed okay that Michael and I were going to do this—just he and I. But the thought of other people investing in the vision created a level of pressure and fear in me I had never felt.

One day in the RV, I had a breakdown. I began to cry and told Michael I just couldn't do this anymore. I asked him to call the realtor (which happened to be my mom) and take the house off the market. I was convinced at that moment that I was going to be known as the woman God blessed but then she thought she had some "vision" and lost everything. I was truly spinning in fear and feelings of inadequacy.

Michael, being the calm force that he is, said to me, "Yes, baby, it is a big thing. In fact, it's a really big thing. But why don't you ask God to confirm for you if this is His idea or yours."

I knew he was right. If God truly called us to this, it would happen. If it wasn't Him calling us to it, I knew He'd confirm that too. We humbly bowed our heads and asked God to give us a Gideon moment.

If you're not familiar with the story of Gideon, he was a man recorded in the Old Testament of the Bible who was asked to do something bigger than himself. Something he didn't feel equipped at all to do. Although he felt it was God asking him to do it, he too wanted to make sure. So he prayed and asked God to confirm that it was Him who was in charge. He specifically asked God to prove it was Him by setting out a fleece (a piece of material made out of animal skin). Gideon asked that when the dew settled on everything, if the fleece be wet but the ground dry, then he would know that it was God. And sure enough, God did that for him.

But I think Gideon is like most of us; he wanted to make sure that wasn't a fluke. He wanted to double check the confirmation. He approached God again and prayed that this time God would do the opposite. He'd send the dew but only on the ground. So the end result would be that the fleece was dry but the ground was wet. And God was gracious enough to do that too. And Gideon went on to do what he was meant to do (Judges 6:36-40).

After our own "fleece request" prayer, I didn't feel any better but had to move on because I had a talk that day in College Station, Texas. It was an "add on" city to the speaking tour. My friend, Nancy, had seen that I was going to be in two cities close by and asked if we could add them to the tour.

She said, "I don't even care what Kathrine is talking about. I just want her to come."

That day we headed to the event venue and I was full of fear. But I wanted to do a good job for my friend so I took a deep breath and walked in. I did the talk as always except that I was dreading the part about Pure Hope Ranch–nervous that I would see the same emotional response and sure enough, I did.

There was a group of young women in the front row that seemed especially touched. They started crying, whispering and passing notes. I wanted to run out of the room. When I was finished speaking, they asked me to come over and talk with them. I went to be polite but what I really wanted to do was bolt. The first thing they said was, "We are so sorry for crying and passing notes while you were still speaking."

I immediately cut them off, trying to coach them in a different direction and give them some additional lessons when they cut me off. "No, you don't understand," they said, "we are all victims of sex trafficking and we need a place exactly like the one you want to start. We know your ranch won't be ready in time to help us but now we know that God sees us and He will take care of us. If He broke your heart with women you didn't even know, surely He will provide us a place."

I was floored. My friend, Nancy, had no idea I would be talking about trafficking in my talk but "just felt led" to invite these young women to the talk. Talk about confirmation. Then they said something to me I will never forget. "Kathrine, thank you. Terrible things happened to us every day while we were trafficked but the worst part was thinking no one cared."

I couldn't even fathom what they went through, and it broke my heart that they would go through their days with that much pain and think no one cared! We now call those women our "front row fleece girls" because God used them to confirm the calling on our lives.

When Michael walked up afterwards, not having any idea of what just happened, I said to him, "Until our last day and our last dollar, we are doing this!"

He said, "What happened? You're like a whole different person."

I briefly told him the story and ended with, "So call my mom and tell her to put the house back on the market."

And he said, "Baby, I never called your mom. I knew God would answer you."

But the story doesn't end there. We went on with our road trip and a few days later "landed" at our friends, Rusty and Joe Armstrong's, ranch just over the border of Texas in New Mexico. We quickly unloaded, ready to stretch our legs after the long drive. Hannah quickly jumped on a horse to ride and Michael walked off talking with Joe. I stood there looking at the beautiful sunset over the mountains, praising God for His faithfulness. Just moments later a gorgeous husky walked up to me followed by an equally gorgeous young woman. I asked her, "Is this your dog?"

She replied, "Yes."

And then I asked, "How do you know Rusty and Joe?"

She responded, "I actually know their son, but I am a survivor of sex trafficking and I have a dream to have a place where women can be fully restored."

WHAT?!? I am here, virtually in the middle of nowhere, I just met this woman and she is reflecting the summary of my vision back to me within minutes of meeting her.

I just looked up in awe of God and I heard Him whisper, "You asked me for a Gideon, Kathrine. I gave him two confirmations. I'm giving you two, too."

Even as I write this I am shaking with awe and joy at the goodness of God. He did not have to do that for me. He could have asked me to completely and blindly walk in faith. But He was gracious enough to give me what I needed. He is good that way.

Interrupted by a Place

We left Rusty and Joe's full of confirmation and passion but with no clear direction. We had looked at several properties while we were on the road trip from Arizona to South Carolina but nothing felt like "the land God would show us." We either liked the structure but not the land or didn't like the areas we looked in. As happy as I was to have the confirmation, I was a little frustrated to not have a clear plan. Our house had not sold either, so it felt like we'd come home and were at a standstill.

I went back to my prayer chair every morning, looking for some revelation or direction. I got nothing. I continued to pray but was getting a little whiney. I would say things to God like, "I know you want us to do this. I just don't know how it's going to happen. Please tell me how God. How is this going to happen? How? How? How?"

Then He responded with a little riddle (He's fun like that with me sometimes) He said, "Rearrange the letters, Kathrine."

Rearrange the letters? H-O-W It took me a moment but then I got it, "It's not HOW, it's WHO. I get it, God, you're going to do this. Then what do you want me to do? I don't know what to do."

And I felt Him respond, "Do what you do know to do."

What did I know to do? The only thing I knew at the time is that God had commissioned me into ministry at the Selah retreat. I knew God put on Michael's heart that the property would be over 1000 acres. I knew how to do the Juice Plus business, run my personal development business and how to help businesses and ministries with strategies. So, when my friends, Mary and Dave Gothi from Significant Marriage called me to have a strategy session, I said yes. They came over to our home and noticed the "For Sale" sign and asked, "Why is your house on the market?"

Remember, everyone that knew me, knew my intention was to "live there until I was 80 years old, looking out that window at the willow tree." I quickly shared with them about the vision of the ranch and Mary responded, "I know the perfect place."

I responded, "What? Where?"

"In Texas," she replied. Well, that got Michael's attention. Although we were willing to go anywhere in the United States, Michael was secretly hoping the "land God would show us" would be in Texas.

We asked her where in Texas it was and she replied that she was not sure. She had friends that went there a couple of times a year to do a grief ministry. She called them and they just happened to be on the property at that moment. I mean, come on, out of 365 days a year, they only go there six days a year and they happen to be there when we called. What are the chances? Mary spoke to Dave briefly and then hung up the phone. She opened her laptop to bring up the website of the ranch and that is when we saw it. SELAH. Selah was the name of the ranch. The same word that was the theme of the yoga retreat where God had commissioned me into ministry. And then we scrolled down and saw that it was 1016 acres. Over 1000 acres just like God had put on Michael's heart. Everything about this place seemed perfect. Each picture on the website was more spectacular than the last. We both had tears in our eyes. Later we saw the price of the ranch and cried more–this time not because we were excited but because it was so much more than we could afford. We had been blessed but not that blessed.

Still, we felt like we just had to connect with the owners. It took a couple of weeks but Michael finally got ahold of Dave and Candy. We briefly explained why we were calling and quickly disclosed that we did not have the kind of money it would take to buy the ranch but just wanted to hear more about it. They graciously invited us out to see the property, to meet them and hear their story. I was already planning a trip back to Texas to work again with Kathy Crockett so we just added a couple of days to the trip so we could take a drive to see it and meet Dave and Candy.

When we pulled onto the property just a few weeks later, Michael and I grabbed hands and started crying. There is no way to describe the connection and peace we felt. The further we drove onto the land, the more beautiful it got and the more overwhelmed I felt. I was struggling because it felt like "the land I will show you," but I also knew the price tag and that there was no way Michael and I could afford it. We decided not to worry about that for the moment but to enjoy seeing the property and meeting the owners. Dave and Candy greeted us at the door of their home and as we stepped in, again I was overwhelmed. It was so much like the vision I had. It was a place of abundant beauty, rich colors and incredibly peaceful.

We all sat down for a beautiful dinner and began to share our stories. We went first, with Dave and Candy listening attentively. I shared about the man on the plane, how God broke my heart over broken families and trafficking and how we had put our home on the market in faith to "go to a land" that God would show us. Candy looked at me with tears in her eyes and said, "You know this is it, don't you? This land is the land, isn't it?"

I started crying and said, "Yes, I think it is, but I don't know how that is possible because we don't have that kind of money."

She responded, "I don't know how either but God does." And then they went on to share their journey (which would make for an incredible book). She ended by saying, "Here's the crazy part. Over the last two years, God has broken my and Dave's heart over the issue of trafficking."

I think we all went to bed that night in deep prayer. Michael was very talkative that night about the possibilities and plans of God and, for once, I was the quiet one. Michael was sure that this was it and that somehow God was going to make this happen. To this day, he has never lost that faith. (At the time I am writing this book, we have not acquired the ranch yet. We have launched the ministry and raised enough money to buy and renovate a home in the same town as the ranch, the Hope Home. We have hired and trained staff and are currently serving victims of trafficking, while we actively, yet patiently - most days - wait on the Lord for the next steps regarding the ranch.)

Interrupted by a Snake

Most people ask us how we raised funds to buy our first Hope Home. That's quite a story. As I went out continuing to speak, there were a few situations that formed our fundraising campaign. I was determined to not just be conformed to the box of traditional fundraising but to ask God for provision and any vision He had that would inspire people to give. One weekend I hosted a women's retreat with my friend, Wendy, and a group of lovely lake home owners on Lake Lanier in Ohio. This was not a fundraising event. It was a faith-based personal development workshop but when it was done the wonderful women that attended handed me an envelope with a collective donation, even though I never made a request. It was a beautiful provision from God.

Then we got back on the road to the next few stops on our tour. About three weeks later I received a private message on Facebook from a woman that said something like, "You may not remember me but I attended the women's retreat in Ohio a few weeks back. When they told us all about Pure Hope Foundation and gave us an opportunity to give, I felt a strong sense from God that I was supposed to give a certain amount of money. I texted my husband and told him about your ministry and asked if I could give a donation. He said yes and I asked him, 'How much?' and he responded, 'Whatever you think.' He didn't know God had put on my heart to give a thousand dollars. I reached for my checkbook to write a check and found I had left it at home. My heart sank and I ended up just giving all the cash I had in my wallet.

She continued, "I went home and it was really bothering me. Why had God put that amount on my heart if I didn't have my checkbook with me? A few weeks passed and my husband came home from work. He said, 'You know those amazing people that will come into the furniture store (where he works) and buy a couch but then buy a second one and tell us that someone will come in today that needs a couch but can't afford it, give that one to them. Well, they came in today and handed me this envelope to give to you.' I opened the card and one thousand dollars fell out and the card said, 'You will know what to do with this.' Of course, I immediately knew to forward it on to you."

I was in awe once again. What a beautiful gift of God and three families were a part of the story. About a month later, I was speaking at a business event. Again, nothing said about the ministry except in my bio. At the end of the talk, a woman walked up to me, handed me a check and said, "I don't normally say things like this but I feel like God wants me to give you this exact amount of money." It was a check for $1000. (Thank you, Mary Jo Stackhouse for stepping out in faith, for your generosity and being part of the miracle!)

A few weeks following that, Michael and I were hosting a marriage retreat and a couple came up to us and said, "Each of us was praying separately about supporting your ministry monthly. We came together and God had given us the same amount of money. We would like to commit to giving you a thousand dollars a month." Once again, God was showing off. (Thank you, Lee and Anita Dickson for your generosity and continued support!)

Then, while on a trip to Selah to visit Dave and Candy and host an event there, I couldn't sleep one night and I kept trying to figure out how many 1000s were in one million (Michael says I shouldn't share that as it was a simple math problem but I'll use the excuse that I was really tired so my brain just wasn't working that night.) When I got up the next morning, Candy said to me, "Last night I was lying in bed trying to figure out how many thousands are in one million."

Of course, I said, "Oh my gosh, me too!"

Right then Dave walked in the room and we asked, "Dave, how many thousands are in one million?" He quickly answered 1000. It was very clear that God was trying to tell me that 1000 was a significant number for us.

I held that in my heart and prayed, "Ok, God, what do you want me to do with this?" No thought or strategy came to mind so I just let it go. We went to visit Michael's parents' lake house for a visit. I went out walking one morning, put on my headphones and was just walking and worshipping when I felt God say, "Turn around and look down." I did and saw a huge snake coiled up in the middle of the pathway that I just walked by. I felt God say, "There is real danger but if you look up and worship me, you will walk right by it and it will not harm you." I have to say my heart was beating like crazy but I was so grateful to God for keeping me safe and teaching me this lesson.

I just had to call someone and tell them so I called my friend, Genia. Once I told her the story she said, "Did I ever tell you about what Mark Burnett and Roma Downing said about snakes while they were filming *The Bible* movie? The morning of the crucifixion screening they had to bring in a snake handler because there were so many snakes at the bottom of the cross."

We continued to talk and she went on to say, "Did I show you a picture of the cute gate at the entrance of my friend's home?"

I said no and she sent over a picture of a simple, yet beautiful, white picket fence. It had a little bronze plaque on the front of it. The saying was in Irish. I asked Genia if she knew what it meant and she said, "One thousand welcomes." Oh! There it was! I remembered the front row fleece girls saying "The worst part was thinking no one cared." And I knew right then what our fundraising campaign was to be. For every person, family, church or organization that donated $1000 we would have a brick paver made with "Welcome Home from…" on the brick. Then we would build a pathway to the home with those bricks so that when the young women arrived at the Hope Home, they would see all the people that cared and were happy that they were home.

Interrupted by a Church Guest

I continued to share the story of what God was doing and one day was asked to be a guest speaker at a small church in San Clemente. One of my greatest blessings is to share my testimony in a church and give the pastor the "day off" to spend time with his family. This particular church was tiny and many of the members were surfers. This is important to the story because this particular Sunday, the waves were exceptionally good so attendance that day was sparse. (Surf church was happening instead)

One lesson I have learned over the years is that the size of the audience does not matter, it is what God wants to do that day and the reception of the hearts of those listening that matters. As I shared the issue of trafficking and my story, I could see people responding. When I was done, there was a small crowd of women gathered around me filled with questions and comments. As I spoke with them, I noticed a woman off to the side. I felt God speak to my heart, "If she tries to leave, go after her."

I took a quick break from answering the other women's questions of the other women to walk over and say to her, "Don't leave." She shyly looked down and nodded. I finished with the group of ladies and finally was alone with the mysterious beautiful blonde with the bright blue eyes. She began, "Thank you for your talk. It meant a lot to me. God told me to come to this church today even though I have my own church. When I walked in and saw how few people were here, I almost left. But I knew I was supposed to stay. When they introduced you, I knew why. I have never told anyone this. Even my mom and children do not know, but twenty years ago I was trafficked. I finally escaped and with a lot of hard work, have built a great life. But I have always known that one day God would call me to make a difference in this issue. I believe that time is now and somehow I am supposed to partner with you."

Since that time, Sonya shared with her mother and children what happened to her. There has been another layer of beauty and healing to her story. She has been an incredible resource and gift to me personally. She continues to partner with Pure Hope Foundation to make a difference. You never know how God is going to guide and direct your life. He will bring you the perfect partners to further His purpose for all involved.

Interrupted by an Acre of Land

Once we knew God was calling us to the area of Selah Ranch, we were just waiting for our home to sell which it did a few months later. As you know, we packed up, put everything in storage and headed to Texas. We didn't know where we were going to live, but we had our RV and Dave and Candy said we could park on Selah Ranch until we found a place.

We began to look for land in the area so we could build or a house on land that we could buy. We could not find anything that worked for us. After a couple of months, Dave and Candy came to us with a portion of Selah that could be easily sectioned off to sell to us. I went to look at it and fell in love. One of my favorite sceneries is rolling pastures with a lone oak tree or two and this piece of property was just that.

We were all ready to buy the land when our plans were interrupted. We came to realize that the acre that fronted our land belonged to another man. We also found out that for the past two decades he was adamant that he did not want to sell it. For years, people had tried to buy it from him and he always said no. And, in fact, we were told he was unwavering and did not even want to discuss it. But you know Michael, he never believes in a closed door until he's done praying. Plus, he's always up for a challenge. He began to pray and then found out where the man lived and dropped by.

Michael walked up to his porch and introduced himself. He let Thomas know that we were considering buying a piece of property from Dave and Candy but would need to buy the acre he owned too because it would be the entrance to our property. Thomas quickly said he was not interested in selling and Michael said, "Well, I understand that Thomas, but will you think about it? Maybe even a way we can pay some sort of easement right so we can put our driveway there?" Thomas quickly replied that he had no interest in selling so Michael left with "Okay, I understand. It was nice to meet you." And he continued to pray.

The next day Michael was driving by and Thomas was walking the acre. Michael stopped and jokingly said, "You walking to see where your property lines are?"

Thomas responded, "Well, if I'm going to sell it to you, I need to know exactly what I'm selling."

Michael quickly said, "I have a surveyor coming over tomorrow to do the property we are buying from Dave and Candy, I'd be happy to have this done also." Thomas agreed. Michael had the survey done. Thomas asked how much per acre we were paying for the land from Dave and Candy. He said, "That will work for me, too." He and Michael shook hands. The next day they were down at the lawyer's office getting papers drawn up and a check was given. It was done. Once again, God made a way when there seemed to be no way.

(Cool side note, Ryan and Holly Morris – who Kathy said would be a part of Pure Hope Foundation when I first shared the vision - joined us in ministry. Ryan is our executive director and Holly serves on our board and in many volunteer capacities. Thomas ended up selling them twenty acres across the street from us and Selah. This was also part of the land that people said they had tried to buy for years but he would not sell. We are so grateful for his willingness and for God's provision.)

Interrupted by a Random Facebook Message

Here's another fun miracle confirmation from God. We had lived in Mount Vernon for a while and had bought the Hope Home. I was still wondering what God was going to do about Selah Ranch. I began to pray and ask God His will. Was this like the Oprah vision–first there would be an open door and part of the vision would come true but then later the full fulfillment would come? Or was the ranch a carrot to get us to settle in this area (which we have no doubt is exactly where God wants us)? There was a season when I began to look at other properties that were more in the price range that Michael and I could purchase on our own. I did that for about three weeks and never had peace when I was doing it. Instead what I felt was stress and pressure. Then one day while I was looking on Realtor.com, I felt God say, "Every time you look at another property, you are committing adultery to the vision I gave you."

I haven't looked at another property since. But just a few short weeks later God gave me an incredible gift through a private Facebook message from a woman I had never met. This is what it said:

"Kathrine, I realize you do not have a clue who I am, and there is a very real risk you may think I am a lunatic, but I need to share something with you. I was born and raised in Mount Vernon and continue to live in the community. About two years ago, I was praying for God to give me a purpose and a very clear understanding of what He wanted me to do to glorify him. I can't even type this without becoming overwhelmed with emotion. God gave me a vision and it was as clear to me as anything I have ever experienced in my life. There are no words I can use to describe it. I went to my husband, Jason, sobbing and said, 'Jason, there is going to be a haven for survivors of sex trafficking and it is going to be Selah Inn. I don't know how or when, but I am positive.'

"My husband is self-employed, business minded and goal-driven to the core, so his natural response was, 'What are we supposed to do to make it happen?" It went against everything in both of our natures to wait, which is exactly what I felt like God was saying for us to do. Wait and pray. There were nights I was so burdened and excited by this 'seed' God had planted in my heart, all I could do was weep.

97

"Flash forward about a year… I was contacted, out of the blue, by an acquaintance who wanted to know if I knew anything about Selah and proceeded to tell me someone was looking to buy Selah and it was an organization to help victims of sex trafficking.

"After staring at the message in complete disbelief, I closed my office door, and dropped to my knees in praise. Again, all I could do was weep and thank God for His faithfulness. There is something so intimate and reassuring about knowing a promise from God is being fulfilled. The scripture, Numbers 23:9, played through my mind. "God is not a man, that He should lie; neither the son of man, that He should repent: hath He said it, and shall He not do it? Or hath He spoken, and shall He not make it good?'

"A few days ago, I stumbled upon your name on Facebook. I have debated and prayed about whether or not to share all of this with you. There is always an element of fear when God beckons us to step outside of our comfort zone and become vulnerable to the rejection of others. However, I am confident God will never lead me in a direction contrary to His will and purpose, and, if nothing else, he demands my obedience, so here it is…

"Kathrine, I still have no idea why God planted this in my heart. I do know, with absolute certainty, what you are doing is ordained by God, it is according to His purpose, and it will come to fruition. It will be by His design, and no one else's. He will provide and move in the midst of situations which seem impossible by human standards. He will draw in faithful servants who are obedient to furthering his kingdom work. It will be the birthplace of mighty spiritual warriors and no weapon formed against it shall prosper. Most importantly, it will ALL be for His glory.

"He wants you to move forward with confidence, wholly trusting in Him, and place your doubts into the sea of forgetfulness. HE has chosen YOU. Guard your ears and heart against those who appear trustworthy, but seek to destroy. In closing, I cannot tell you how excited I am about this anointed ministry! If I can help you in any way, please feel free to contact me. I am a licensed social worker by profession, but my first love is serving in whatever capacity God directs me. I will continue to pray vigilantly for you and hold you dear to my heart. Thank you, thank you, thank you for your willingness to step into the unknown. Sincerely, Nicole W."

Needless to say, Nicole, and her husband Jason, have become great friends and invaluable partners in this ministry.

Interrupted by a Worshipper

God continued to direct the way I invested my time. I consistently had to make decisions about where and when to travel. What to say yes and no to. I've been blessed to get lots of requests for speaking and each time I prayed and asked God if this was a trip I should take. There was one particular women's group in Ohio that had been asking me for nine years to come speak for them and the timing was never right until July of 2015. This time when they asked, I felt it was time to say yes.

The morning of the talk I walked in and a woman passed me. I didn't see her directly—just the back of her as she went down the hallway. It was the strangest feeling, as if God was highlighting her to me. I entered into the main meeting room where I would be speaking. They explained the flow of the morning and told me I would be going on after the worship singer.

When they began the morning and introduced the woman who would be leading us in a worship song the woman I passed in the hallway stood up and went to the piano. After the first notes she played on the piano, I felt like I was being transported right to the throne room of God (and that is not a phrase I ever use). It was an incredibly powerful experience. Her voice was beautiful but it was more than that. There was a distinct difference in the way she sang. It was as if she wasn't a worship leader but instead a worshipper.

I went on right after her, completely at peace but also with a greater passion to impart what God had given me to share that day. When I was done, she ran up to me and said, "Can you wait just a few minutes? I have to talk with you. I just need to run get my daughter out of childcare and I will be right back."

I talked with other women until she returned and then she said something that surprised but thrilled me. She began, "I don't want this to sound weird. I am usually not a self-promoter or this bold, but all of my life I knew I was going to have 'a person' that I would be the worship leader for. It would be someone that was a speaker and I would be the one to lead worship for her. Kind of like Beth Moore and Travis Cottrell. When you walked up on stage, before you ever spoke a word, I felt God say, 'She's your person.'" Right then, as I was taking that in, she called for her daughter, "Selah, come here." What?!? Her daughter's name was Selah. The same word that was used when I felt God commission me into ministry and the name of the "land God showed us." Once again I stood in awe of God.

Natalie Runion has since written an incredible original song along with Craig Aven and performed with David and Amanda Lessing. It is called *God of My Rescue* (available on iTunes) and they are working on an entire album to benefit Pure Hope Foundation. Natalie not only is one of the most talented singers I know, but has an incredible heart for God and a passion to make a difference in the realm of trafficking. And she's a whole lot of fun. She is "my person."

God of My Rescue

From the fire You saved me. Shield me from the flame.

Stand beside me, whispering my name.

In the night, when I'm trembling in the dark,

You hold on tight. I find refuge in Your arms.

You're the God of my rescue; I won't be afraid.

My Savior, Redeemer, You pulled me from the grave.

So come what may, You will see me through.

You're the God of my rescue.

You quiet the waters, and the wind will obey.

At the sound of Your Word, Jesus, at the mention of Your Name.

My enemies all tremble when You speak.

They see you standing at my guard and fall before me in defeat.

You're the God of my rescue; I won't be afraid.

My Savior, Redeemer, You pulled me from the grave.

So come what may, You will see me through.

You're the God of my rescue.

Like Daniel in the lion's den, David in the field,

Like Paul and Silas singing in their chains,

Like the Hebrew boys rejoicing from the center of the flames,

I'm standing in the power of Your Name.

You're the God of my rescue; I won't be afraid.

My Savior, Redeemer, You pulled me from the grave.

So come what may, You will see me through.

You're the God of my rescue.

You're my God. You're my God. You're the God of my rescue.

Interrupted by an Artist

One of the lessons I have learned over the years is to make worship and prayer my number one priority. When I don't, I get stressed, confused and angry. I don't know why anger always creeps in when I forget who God is but it is always the case. Maybe because fear sounds like anger and when I have forgotten that God is in control (which is what I am always reminded of when I worship and pray) I become afraid and it feels more powerful to be angry than scared. But when I pray, not only do I experience peace and clarity, but I also experience love which, for me, is the opposite of feeling anger. And when I pray, God guides me. I always seem to know what to say yes to and what to say no to when I pray.

One pattern in the way God guides me is to bring something up many times from many different directions. At the beginning of 2015, Bethel Church in Redding, California, kept coming up from various sources. These were random locations from people that were not connected. A friend would give me a book that was from one of the Bethel staff. Another person would tell me about their experience there. Still another would send me a song on YouTube that was sung by the worship team at Bethel. I finally prayed, "Ok, God, it seems like You're wanting me to know more about Bethel. I even feel a sense that You want me to go there. If that's You, please make it obvious."

A couple of weeks later, I headed to Sacramento, California to speak for the Juice Plus Company. The talk was a business talk and did not include my faith as part of the content. Yet, when the talk was over this man walked up to me with a couple of other women and said, "I know you didn't mention God in your talk, but the minute you started talking I felt Him through you." He went on to add, "I am a pastor at a church and we would love to host you there sometime."

He held out his card. As I took it, I immediately saw Bethel Church, Redding, California. I began to laugh and explained to him what God had been doing regarding his church and added, "I'd love to come visit."

A few months later I headed back to Northern California with some wonderful friends, but this time it was to visit Bethel. Ken Williams, the pastor I had met at the event months prior, did an amazing job hosting us. We got to meet and connect with several different ministry leaders there and were blessed by each connection. Ken explained to me that he had a special time planned for us with a group of people that had been praying for us even before we came. They didn't know anything about us; they were just given our names. When we arrived in the room, each of us got to spend time with a specific group of people that were "assigned" to pray for us. It was such a blessing.

Then they gathered us together. Displayed in the front of the room was a small grouping of items. There was a painting on an easel, a chair, and a few other items. The painting immediately caught my eye. It was a group of different kinds of shoes. Kind of like what you would find inside a front door of someone's home, as if the family came home and took off their shoes in the entry way. There were tennis shoes, kids' shoes, men's business shoes, red high heels and a pair of black patent leather army boots in the middle. It was those boots that caught my eye. They looked exactly like a pair I own.

But here's the amazing thing, those boots were very significant to me. Why? Because when I began to go out and speak about trafficking, I felt God tell me to wear those boots every time I spoke on the issue. He reminded me of that time in the living room all those years before where He spoke, "This is a war, build the armies." So, each time I spoke, I put on those army boots and there they were in the painting. And then I saw the name of the painting, "Welcome Home." I was stunned. Remember the "1000 Welcomes Campaign"? And the pavers that said, "Welcome Home"? Two very significant pieces of my journey were contained in that painting. I felt I needed to own it. The artist was there in the room so I asked her if I could get her contact information. I told her how special the painting was to me but none of the details of why. I let her know that I would like to connect while I was in town if that was possible.

The next morning, I felt led to text her and God even gave me the specific words: "I would like to know how much the investment would be to have the privilege of owning the painting." She quickly responded that God had told her that morning that she was to give it to me as a gift and explained what the painting represented. She said it symbolized that no matter where we have been we are welcome to come home. We made a plan to meet that day as I felt I needed to explain to her the significance of the army boots and the meaning of the name "Welcome Home."

We met at the coffee shop at Bethel, her carrying the painting and me bringing a story of how powerfully God had used her gift. As I shared with her about the

1000 Welcomes Campaign, the purpose of Pure Hope Foundation (to strengthen families and restore victims of trafficking) she had tears in her eyes. Then I shared with her the significance of the army boots and she gasped. "Kathrine, when I asked God what to paint, the first thing He gave me was the army boots. They were the first thing I painted and the rest came after that."

Interrupted by a 1-inch Rendering

As we continued to move forward with the Hope Home opening and wonderful things began happening to strengthen families, the fulfillment of the vision of the ranch was stilling tugging at my heart every day. We were practically pursuing the "normal" means for a project this big but I also felt led that my most important role was, and will always be, to "seek God's face" in prayer through worship. I know that when I seek His face, His will and way open up before me.

Recently as I was praying about next steps in the process of receiving the land, I felt God say, "It's time to have an artist rendering of the vision." To be honest, I knew that was God because I really didn't know what an artist rendering was. But I could see it in my mind. It would be a water color, bird's eye view of the property as it is and with the different areas of the vision developed. So, of course, I went to locate an artist that I could get to create something like that for us. But as I went to go pursue that, I felt God say, "Don't do anything about it."

"What? Don't do anything? But You just said to get an artist rendering done," I responded in confusion.

"No, I didn't say to get one done. I said it was time." Still confused, I sat in silence pondering what that meant. It was time, but I was not to do anything. "Ok, God. I trust you. Tell me when You want me to do something."

Weeks went by. I told our team I felt that was the next step but didn't tell them I wasn't going to do anything about it because that just didn't make sense. I have to admit, there were times I asked people if they knew anyone that did them. I even went to Google a few times to look for someone, but each time I did, I felt this sense of disobedience, so I would stop.

Then one weekend, I was headed to Mimi Lee's (my mother-in-law's) home for a visit. She and I work together in the Juice Plus company and she had asked if I would come down and do a dream board training for her community. I love guiding people to pray and ask God to reveal the desires of their hearts and then translate in pictures what comes to mind. That evening we had a small group of people gather at a darling art studio and gift shop (Across the Tracks) in Livingston, Texas. I explained to them how to construct a dream board and they went to work.

When everyone was done, I went around looking at each one. It is so fun to see how unique each persons' comes out. Some people only have a few pictures, others have lots of words, some have just one theme like travel, others cover a variety of topics.

I went over to one woman who was still diligently working. Her entire poster board was covered and she was still adding to it. It was so creative and beautiful. As I looked at it, one small square stood out to me. "What's that?" I asked.

She responded, "That's an artist rendering of a property we want to develop."

God whispers, "See why you didn't have to do anything? I already had her in mind."

She introduced herself as Tamara Crossly. I quickly found out she was a very talented artist, as much of her work was displayed in the building we were in. I asked her if she would be interested in doing a rendering for me and she said yes. We made plans to meet the next day.

I went to meet with her at her home the next day and was honored to see more of her work, meet her beautiful girls and enjoy some homemade shortbread that one of them made. It was an amazing visit and at the end she told me she would be honored to do the rendering on one condition, that it could be a gift. I told her, "No way, my daughter is an artist and I know how hard you all work and the heart you put in. I insist on paying you." She held her ground and I finally conceded.

She came out to visit the ranch, asked me more clarifying questions and went to work. When she sent me the rendering I was stunned! It was more than we could ever have asked or imagined. She not only made an overview painting but also made separate "blow ups" of each section. She also included a 3-inch binder full of the research she had compiled for each area of development. For instance, she researched every aspect of the eco-therapy garden (what types of flowers and plants grow best in the region, which ones attracted butterflies, etc.) and did the same with each section. Ephesians 3:20 promises that "God is able to do immeasurably more than all we ask or imagine" and Tamara is a living example of that to me.

Interrupted by a Text

This last story is actually happening right now. I am in the story this very minute. Before I tell you where I am, let me go back and tell you how I got here.

Just a week ago, Genia came out to visit. We spent two days at Selah having friendship, prayer and strategy time. At the end of the trip, Genia and I committed to block off the following week to write. I told her I would but felt like I needed a place with an expansive view to inspire me. I thought maybe someone around our area would have a lake house I could use. Genia also kept saying that she felt like we needed to find a model of a family camp and disc golf course and study their model. And the funny thing is, she kept saying, "I keep hearing from God, 'There's gold in them hills.'" (and she said it with a Texas accent). She must have repeated that three or four times before she left. It was always followed by, "I know it doesn't make any sense because there are not hills here but I just keep hearing it."

The afternoon that she left, I came back home and got on Facebook just to see what the rest of the world was doing. I came across another post from my friends, Randall and Dana Popham. They had been posting pictures all week from the retreat they were attending. But something was different this time when I saw the photo. It was like the place jumped off the page at me. I clicked on the link to Wind River Ranch.

I immediately knew it was the model we were to look at. I quickly sent a message to Dana, asking her to call me when she got home. I explained to her about what Genia said and that I felt I needed to know as much about the ranch as possible. Dana has visited Selah so I just knew she was the perfect person to share with me what she saw in common between the two ranches. I then sent a voice message and link to the ranch to Ryan, Holly and Michael, explaining that I felt like it was the perfect place for us to look at. Those messages were sent at 4:41 and 4:43. At 4:58 I received a text from a woman, Vanessa O'Neal, that had come to one of our retreats at Selah. Vanessa said they were still looking for speakers for a retreat for a group that was coming (City of Refuge Atlanta) and said the retreat was being held in Estes Park, Colorado. I responded back, "What's the location?" She replied at 5:04 p.m., "Wind River Ranch, Estes Park, CO. www.windriverranch.com"

Yes! Fifteen minutes after telling our team we needed to look at Wind River Ranch, they send me an invitation to come to the property! So I am sitting in a cabin right now at Wind River Ranch, with an expansive view of the Rocky Mountains, writing this book. The best part is that for the last four days I've gotten to see a combination of a family camp and restoration of trafficking victims happen at the same time. And that is the exact desire for the future of Selah.

I've heard it said, "I don't know what the future holds, but I know Who holds the future." I have so many things I want you to know but I especially want you to realize that God is real. He is good. He has a plan for your life and He's just waiting for you to join Him in the Mystery of walking it out. Welcome to the Adventure. The best is yet to come.

Corryn, Logan and Hannah,

There are so many more stories but they have to do with you more personally and about our family specifically. Since other people may read this book, I wanted to give you the choice of whether or not those stories would be shared. When you want to hear them, come to me and I will tell you. Then you can decide if you want to share them with others.

I love you more than words can say,

Mom

Scriptures that have guided my life:

For the Lord is a sun and shield, the Lord bestows favor and honor; no good thing does He withhold from those whose walk is blameless. (Psalm 84:11)

Let Your beauty be upon me, and establish the work of my hands. (Psalm 90:17)

You will keep in perfect peace he whose mind is stayed on You, because he trusts in You. (Isaiah 26:3)

God is light, in Him there is no darkness at all. (1 John 1:5)

For God is working in you, giving you the power and desire to do what pleases Him. (Philippians 2:13)

The faithful love of the Lord never ends. His mercies never cease, great is His faithfulness; His mercies begin afresh each morning. (Lamentations 3:22-23a)

Whatever is true, whatever is noble, whatever is right, whatever is pure, whatever is lovely, whatever is admirable – if anything is excellent or praiseworthy - think about such things. (Philippians 4:8)

Oh, the joys of those who do not follow the advice of the wicked, or stand around with sinners, or join in with mockers. But they delight in the law of the Lord, meditating on it day and night; they are like trees planted along the riverbank, bearing fruit in each season. Their leaves never wither, and they prosper in all they do. (Psalm 1:1-3)

The Spirit of the Sovereign Lord is upon me, for the Lord has appointed me to bring good news to the poor. He has sent me to comfort the brokenhearted and proclaim that the captives will be released and prisoners will be freed. He has sent me to tell those who mourn that the time of the Lord's favor has come, and with it, the day of God's anger against their enemies. To all who mourn in Israel He will give a crown of beauty for ashes, a joyous blessing instead of mourning, festive praise instead of despair. In their righteousness, they will be like great oaks that the Lord has planted for His own glory. (Isaiah 61:1-3, NLT)

Cast all your cares on Him because He cares for you. (1 Peter 5:7)

A man's heart plans his way but the Lord directs his steps. (Proverbs 16:9)

Cause me to know the way in which I should walk, for I lift up my soul to you. (Psalm 143:8)

If any of you lacks wisdom, let him ask of God, who gives to all liberally and without reproach, and it will be given to him. (James 1:5)

When He, the Spirit of Truth comes, He will guide you in all truth. (John 16:13)

Be strong and take heart and wait for the Lord. (Psalm 27:14)

The Lord Himself will fight for you; you need only be still. (Exodus 14:14. NIV)

I don't want your sacrifices – I want your love; I don't want your offerings – I want you to know Me. (Hosea 6:6, TLB)

Do not become weary in doing good, for at the proper time we will reap a harvest if we do not give up. (Galatians 6:9)

He who began a good work in you will be faithful to complete it. (Philippians 1:6, NIV)

Delight yourself in the Lord and He will give you the desires of your heart. (Psalm 37:4)

The Lord directs the steps of the godly, He delights in every detail of their lives. Though they may stumble, they will never fall, for the Lord holds them by the hand. (Psalm 37:23-24)

In the morning, Lord, You hear my voice; in the morning I lay my requests before You and wait expectantly. (Psalm 5:3)

You will seek Me and find Me when you seek Me with all of your heart. (Jeremiah 29:13, NIV)

Ask and it will be given to you; seek and you will find; knock and the door will be opened to you. For everyone who asks receives, and he who seeks finds, and to him who knocks the door will be opened. (Matthew 7:7-8, NIV)

My heart says of you, "Seek His face!" Your face, Lord, I will seek. (Psalm 27:8, NIV)

But if God so clothes the grass of the field, which is alive today and tomorrow is thrown into the furnace, will He not much more clothe you? You of little faith! Do not worry then, saying, "What will we eat?' or 'What will we drink?' or 'What will we wear for clothing?' For the Gentiles eagerly seek all these things; for your heavenly Father knows that you need all these things. But seek first His Kingdom and His righteousness, and all these things will be added to you. So do not worry about tomorrow; for tomorrow will take care of itself. Each day has enough trouble of its own.   (Matthew 6:30-34, NASB)

Whatever your hand finds to do, do it with all of your might. (Ecclesiastes 9:10)

The Lord has done great things for us and we are filled with joy. (Psalm 126:3)

Why would I fear the future? For I am being pursued only by Your goodness and unfailing love. (Psalm 23:6)

Wait for the Lord; be strong, and let your heart take courage; wait for the Lord. (Psalm 27:24)

You will be secure because there is hope; you will look about you and take your rest in safety. You will lie down, with no one to make you afraid. (Job 11:18-19)

I will exalt you, O Lord for You lifted me out of the pit and did not let my enemies gloat over me. O Lord my God, I called to You for help and You healed me. O Lord, You brought me up from the grave; You spared me from going down into the pit. Sing to the Lord, you saints of His; praise His holy name. For His anger lasts only a moment, but His favor lasts a lifetime; weeping may remain for a night but joy comes in the morning. When I felt secure I said, "I will never be shaken," O Lord, when You favored me, You made my mountain stand firm. But when You hid your face, I was dismayed. To You, O Lord, to the Lord I cried for mercy; what gain is there if I am silenced, in my going down into the pit? Will my dust praise You? Will it proclaim Your faithfulness? Hear, O Lord, and be merciful to me; O Lord be my help. You turned my wailing into dancing; You removed my sackcloth and clothed me with joy, that my heart may sing to You and not be silent, O Lord, my God, I will give You thanks forever. (Psalm 30:1-12)

Arise, shine, for your light has come, and the glory of the Lord has risen upon you. (Isaiah 60:1, NIV)

You are the God who performs miracles. You display Your power among the peoples. (Psalm 77:14, NIV)

Whether you turn to the right or to the left, your ears will hear a voice behind you, saying, "This is the way; walk in it." (Isaiah 30:21, NIV)

If My people, who are called by My name, will humble themselves and pray and seek My face and turn from their wicked ways, then I will hear from heaven, and I will forgive their sin and will heal their land. (2 Chronicles 7:14, NIV)

Commit your work to the Lord and your plans will be established. (Proverbs 16:3)

Trust in the Lord with all your heart and lean not on your own understanding; in all your ways acknowledge Him, and He shall direct your paths. (Proverbs 3:5-6)

Lessons I've learned along the way that I want you to know:

Never give up childlike faith. God wants to reveal things to you but you will not see them if you look at the world through the critical, logical and/or cynical eyes of adulthood. (Corryn, remember the time by the lake when God revealed to you that He was the greatest artist of all? Logan, never forget the time when you were three years old and Jesus "came in your room and taught you all the scriptures." Remember how beautiful you said He was? And Hannah, remember the day in the Polaris on the land when you had the "perfect moment"? All of these were times in which God was revealing Himself personally to each of you.

Our faith cannot come second hand. I think this is why I have not been as bold about my faith to you until now. I never wanted you to look to me for the Truth but rather to the One that is the Truth. I am sharing with you now so you can see the tangible evidence in my life that He is real and I pray you will spend time getting to know Him more for yourselves.

Please don't look at me or any other Christian as the standard for choosing and following Christ. Look at Him. Read about Him in the Bible. Study the things He said and the actions He took. I know He will reveal Himself to you in a very personal way.

Nothing can fill the void that only God can.

Love is not about an initial thrill or connecting to someone out of brokenness.

We were all designed from the beginning of time with a purpose in mind.

God can take any of our pain and turn it to purpose.

Live expectantly.

Believe in miracles.

Seek God's face, and His will and His way will open up before you.

Please don't choose a spouse out of brokenness. Let God love you and choose from a place of wholeness.

God is meant to fill a certain part of our hearts that no person can.

God can choose to give great gifts, the greatest gifts in fact, despite our decisions.

If you lean on God, He will get you through the darkest of times.

If you honor God and His ways, He will reward that in a variety of ways.

Comparison is emotional cancer.

What we perceive as rejection is protection and redirection to something better.

You can be alone but not lonely when you have a relationship with God.

There is a gift waiting for you in the silence.

References:

PureHopeFoundation.com

UltimateSource.tv

Fightthenewdrug.org

Justoneclickaway.org

RedeemedMinistries.com

DreamCenter.org (Project Hope)

JuicePlus.com

Tamyra Crossley (artist that did the rendering of the vision – fineartamerica.com/profiles/Tamyra-Crossley)

Nicola Hill (artist I met at Bethel - @nicolahillartist)

WindRiverRanch.com

God of My Rescue (song can be found on iTunes) Artists: Natalie Runion (nrrunion@gmail.com; CraigAven.com; DavidandAmandaLessingMusic.com)

HatfieldFilms.com

CityofRefugeAtl.org

Made in the USA
Columbia, SC
11 May 2019